# LEARNING TO LOVE A PORCUPINE

# LEARNING TO LOVE A PORCUPINE

*Hope for Drug Addicts*
*—— and Families in Crisis ——*

BOB McLEOD

Copyrighted Material

Learning to Love a Porcupine: Hope for Drug Addicts and Families in Crisis

Copyright © 2020 by BrokenStone Ministries. All Rights Reserved.

No part of this publication may be reproduced, stored in a retrieval system or transmitted, in any form or by any means—electronic, mechanical, photocopying, recording or otherwise—without prior written permission from the publisher, except for the inclusion of brief quotations in a review.

For information about this title or to order other books and/or electronic media, contact the publisher:

BrokenStone Ministries
www.Ouch.Love
Bob@Ouch.Love

ISBNs:
978-1-889503-10-3 (hardcover)
978-1-889503-12-7 (color softcover)
978-1-889503-13-4 (black-and-white softcover)
978-1-889503-11-0 (eBook)

Printed in the United States of America

Cover and Interior design: 1106 Design

Special thanks to:
Sherry Kughn, editor
Lizi Leroux, Operations
Mark Hicks Photography
George J. Johnson, OFA Secretary of State

Some of the names have been changed to protect the innocent and the guilty.

# Table of Contents

**Foreword**     xiii
   *Lesson Learned Lyrics: Tryin' to Love a Porcupine*

**Chapter 1   Meek, not Weak**     1
   *Lesson Learned Lyrics: Friendship Rules, The Freedom of Unfailing Love*

**Chapter 2   Our Beloved Bowie**     7
   *Lesson Learned Lyrics: Chinese Custom, Case Sensitive*

**Chapter 3   Nearly Got Hank Jr. Killed**     13
   *Lesson Learned Lyrics: So Help Me God*

**Chapter 4   The Night the Old Man Died**     21
   *Lesson Learned Lyrics: The Night the Old Man Died*

**Chapter 5   God Sent an Angel to Turn a Devil Around**     27
   *Lesson Learned Lyrics: Suffering Love, She Is*

Chapter 6  My Friend, Ken                                              33
   *Lesson Learned Lyrics:* Bug Zapper, Al K. Hall

Chapter 7  Can a Hell Raiser Go to Heaven?                             43
   *Lesson Learned Lyrics:* Hand Grenades and Horseshoes

Chapter 8  Dignitaries and Derelicts                                   51
   *Lesson Learned Lyrics:* Have You Seen Jesus?

Chapter 9  Affection/Rejection Principle                               57
   *Lesson Learned Lyrics:* Let 'um Know That We're Loved

Chapter 10  Nances Creek Detour                                        67
   *Lesson Learned Lyrics:* It Finally Dawned on Me

Chapter 11  Heart Bigger Than Head                                     73
   *Lesson Learned Lyrics:* Rest Assured, Pocket Tees and Lee's

Chapter 12  What Is Our Father's Arms?                                 83
   *Lesson Learned Lyrics:* Let Me Love You

Chapter 13  Life Is a Matter of Perspective                            89
   *Lesson Learned Lyrics:* Perspective

Chapter 14  Where Can Someone Find Sympathy?                           103
   *Lesson Learned Lyrics:* I'd Like to Recommend a Doctor

Chapter 15  500-Pound Man in the Basement                              113
   *Lesson Learned Lyrics:* Reality Road

Chapter 16  The Big Bank                                               123
   *Lesson Learned Lyrics:* Love Not Money

## Table of Contents

Chapter 17  Vance — 131
*Lesson Learned Lyrics: A Life of Love*

Chapter 18  Billy and Nathan — 139
*Lesson Learned Lyrics: No Reputation*

Chapter 19  Mother Millie — 145
*Lesson Learned Lyrics: Eagle With a Broken Wing*

Chapter 20  Freed from Fear — 153
*Lesson Learned Lyrics: Straining on a Gnat*

Chapter 21  Homeless Child — 161
*Lesson Learned Lyrics: Homeless Child*

Chapter 22  He Put Sue Aside — 169
*Lesson Learned Lyrics: A Way with Words*

Chapter 23  The Revelation of Resurrection — 181
*Lesson Learned Lyrics: Afraid of Faith*

Chapter 24  Thank You Therapy — 189
*Lesson Learned Lyrics: Two Words*

Chapter 25  The Light Shined on Me — 195
*Lesson Learned Lyrics: Stop Wasting Our Time*

Chapter 26  USA Gang — 201
*Lesson Learned Lyrics: We Dig Our Own Grave*

Chapter 27  Holman Prison Death Row — 209
*Lesson Learned Lyrics: Unholy Lie, They Don't Know You*

| | |
|---|---|
| Chapter 28  One on One<br>*Lesson Learned Lyrics:* Pity the Man | 219 |
| Chapter 29  Trample on Love<br>*Lesson Learned Lyrics:* Trampled on Love | 225 |
| Chapter 30  Our Father's Arms International<br>*Lesson Learned Lyrics:* Little Flowers | 233 |
| Chapter 31  Dugger Mountain Music Hall<br>*Lesson Learned Lyrics:* Come One, Come All | 243 |
| Chapter 32  Falling in Love With God's Word<br>*Lesson Learned Lyrics:* He Gives His Word | 251 |
| Chapter 33  Making Disciples One Day at a Time<br>*Lesson Learned Lyrics:* Called ID, The Final Analysis | 257 |
| Appendix A: Pacifier or Satisfier<br>*Lesson Learned Lyrics:* Need Inside of Me | 271 |
| Appendix B: The Window<br>*Lesson Learned Lyrics:* Just Look | 279 |

# Learning to Love a Porcupine

## *Hope for Drug Addicts and Families in Crisis*

Bob McLeod

*A real-life story about learning to love the unlovable, even when it hurts.*

# Credits

*Bob, a kite,*
*Abandoned to soar,*
*Free, fearless,*
*Prone to drift and crash.*

*Patti, a string,*
*Anchor, secure, steadfast.*

*Jesus, the Hand Who holds,*
*The Tie that binds,*
*The Wind Who allows us to climb*
*Higher and higher with Him.*
*We love you, Jesus.*

*All credit to You.*
*Thank you for Patti!*

# Foreword

## Tryin' to Love a Porcupine

I want you to know,
There's no way I would hurt you intentionally,
But you take everything I say all wrong
Then you say, "So long!"
How are you going to listen
While you're screaming at me?

You've been hurt so much.
You're not about to let anybody touch you.
Your wounded heart just bleeds and seethes with hate
'Cause you don't think very much of you.

Lovin' you is like Tryin' to Love a Porcupine.
Baby, it's true, nobody can get close to you.

## Learning to Love a Porcupine

*I pray that you'll be healed, in time.*
*But until then, I might as well*
*Try to Love a Porcupine!*

*Jesus is with us, right here,*
*Longing to remove your quills.*
*Stick closer to you than a brother*
*And give you His love*
*So that you can receive love from another*
*But until then,*
*I might as well try to Love a Porcupine! Ouch!*

***–Bob McLeod***

## Foreword

## Dear Reader:

You and I, like it or not, find ourselves living in an insane world of unavoidable suffering, escalating conflicts, terrorism, tormenting fear, grief, betrayal, unbearable heartbreak, and pandemic deadly drug addictions. The stress intensity level is rising and most of the time brought on by insensible, irrational, inconsiderate, difficult, if not impossible-to-get-along-with-people (porcupines), and I'd rather not admit it, but on occasion, the porcupine has been me! Welcome to the rental, mental institution called, Planet Earth!

Is it possible for anyone, in spite of it all, to live day by day, a joyful, peaceful, sober, successful, overcoming life? Is it really possible? We are discovering, most definitely, absolutely YES, though not "in spite of" but surprisingly even, "because of."

The key is unfailing love. We are told in **1st Corinthians 13:8** that *"love never fails."* If that's true, then why do we hear the repeated phrase, *"I love you,"* and, then, just as frequently, hear, *"I don't love you anymore"*? Our contradictory words reveal that what we've been calling "love" is, most of the time, nothing more than a superficial, insecure, deceptive, impotent, counterfeit feeling.

Therefore, if we're to be successful and overcome, that word LOVE must first have a complete redefinition. One must be willing to recognize and unlearn the misconceptions, deceptions, and lies programmed into us by our culture and its earthbound perspective. We humbly trust, hope, and pray that this book will somehow help.

We dare not claim to have mastered the successful, overcoming lifestyle by any means. We continue to stumble, struggle, fall, and mess things up, but less and less, because we are in the glorious process of awakening and coming alive with a newfound hope, freedom, and victory—and there's no way we can stay quiet about that! Hence, this book!

Over the years, music has been the heartbeat of all that we do. Writing songs that help document and communicate the powerful, life-changing lessons that we've been learning has, for decades, been a way of life. Throughout this book, I'll be sharing song lyrics at the end of each chapter. Many of these songs are available to hear and download at www.HopeInHurt.com.

In Our Father's Arms,

*~Bob*

## Counterfeit Love

*He said, "I love you."*
*She wanted to believe.*
*It wasn't love,*
*It was lust.*
*They were both deceived.*
*She aborted their baby,*
*Now he's gone, she's alone, lonely as hell.*
*Counterfeit Love never fails to fail.*

# Foreword

*Counterfeit Love never fails to fail.*
*Counterfeit Love, an empty wishing well.*
*"I don't love you anymore" is how you can tell.*
*Counterfeit Love never fails to fail.*

*He says, "I love you"*
*But you're afraid to commit.*
*You've been so hurt by all of the religious counterfeits.*
*But for there to be a counterfeit,*
*There has to be a real.*
*Betrayed by a kiss,*
*He knows exactly how you feel.*

*Just look to that cross,*
*The crown of thorns, the bloody sword and the nails.*
*It's only there you will find*
*True Love that never, ever fails.*

# CHAPTER 1

## *Meek, Not Weak*

The caller ID said, "private number." I answered it anyway.

"Is this Bob McLeod?"

"Yes, it is. How can I help you?"

"Mr. McLeod, this is Officer Hendrick. I'm an investigator for the City of Jacksonville Police Department. Do you know Lamar Murray?"

"Yes, sir, I know who he is. Why do you ask?"

"It's been reported to us that he said he's coming to kill you. He's armed and dangerous. You need to know, and we need to know where you'll be at all times. He drives a late-model blue Ford truck. Please don't hesitate to call me if you see him. Will you do that?"

"Yes, sir. For sure. Thank you, officer!"

I certainly kept a lookout but never saw Lamar or his truck. However, a week after Officer Hendrick's call, Lamar found out where his ex-wife Julie was living. Ignoring the restraining order, he pulled into her driveway. She calls 911 as he breaks down the door and starts firing. Julie is dead.

The police arrive. Lamar steps out on the front porch with a revolver in each hand and starts firing at the police. They fire back. Lamar is dead.

What led up to all that?

I have worked for several decades with a ministry known as Our Father's Arms (OFA). We are located in the northern part of Calhoun County, Alabama. Part of our mission is to provide homes of healing and hope for individuals and families in crisis.

As early as 1997, Julie, badly beaten, desperate to get away from Lamar, called me and came to live with us at OFA. Disregarding our advice, she would not press charges. She stayed with us only a few days and went back to him. For 21 years, he not only continued to abuse her but also continued to resent and hate me for trying to help her.

Over the years, I have been accused, insulted, blamed, stolen from, lied about, lied to, taken advantage of, condemned, screamed at, and swung at! And Lamar is not the only one. I've been threatened with murder multiple times.

There's been arson, threats of legal "cease and desist" orders, sirens blaring, flashing lights, police cars, handcuffs and arrests, paraphernalia smuggled in for a meth lab, drug overdoses, ambulances, and heartbreaking funerals.

For multiple decades, my wife Patti and I have been bombarded by calls at all hours from frantic, tormented souls desperately begging and often times demanding help.

That's what happens when the word gets out that you will gladly open your heart and home with no money required. It makes us look like we're weak, easy prey. But we don't care what it looks like. We do it anyway!

We're learning that meekness is not weakness. Meekness is "power under control"! Our Lord Jesus on that cross is a perfect example.

# Meek, Not Weak

**Matthew 5:5** "Blessed are the meek"; Patti and I are so blessed, even though often times we may appear to be vulnerable and weak!

*"Don't let them run over you," I hear them say, but what about the Man Who died, hanging on a cross that day? When instead of violence, you bow your head and pray; my son, then my son, you're really a man."*

We are often times hurt, but by God's grace, we're learning to let Him bind up our broken hearts (**Isaiah 61:1**) and simply keep doing what we've been doing, and that certainly means having our hearts broken again and again.

There have been times when our good nature has been mistaken for weakness, and a bully shows up trying to take advantage and even take over. I try not to enjoy seeing him fall!

We never run from or bow to any man. No need to. If God Almighty is for you, then who can be against you? **Romans 8:31**

**Luke 10:19** "Behold, I give unto you power to tread on serpents and scorpions, and over all the power of the enemy: and nothing shall by any means hurt you" is another verse that comes to mind. Whenever anyone crosses mercy's boundary asking for a fight, they never win.

Not always, but sometimes, seemingly out of nowhere, the miracle happens. Light shines into the darkness, and a tormented soul is set free. Families are restored, and children get their mommies and daddies back. Only Almighty God, Who is Love, can do that, and He is allowing us to have part in His glorious redemptive plan.

The dynamic of what's been happening here at OFA is very mysterious and therefore easily misunderstood. We've been called a rehab program and a halfway house, but that's not at all who we are. We are quite simply an extended, Christ-centered family, in many cases providing a place to call home during one's transition from a life of self-destructive turmoil and misery to a life of peace and serenity, a turnaround that can happen in days, or sometimes, it can take years. Together, we are learning to live the freedom of unfailing love.

There are times when we get tired, wounded, feel insecure, broken, so prone and tempted to live in worry, anxiety, and fear. Those times remind us of how much we need our Shepherd. We rest and pray through it, consciously in the process of learning how to receive the unfailing love of our Lord Jesus Christ, a love that forgives, heals, transforms, and, indeed, casts out all fear and eliminates all insecurities, a truth found in **1 John 4:18**.

We are not living fully free yet, but we are personally experiencing an ongoing, glorious awakening that will continue until we exit time and space.

Our Father's Arms is the Residential/Outreach component of BrokenStone Ministries, a 501C3 non-profit founded in 1984.

I had nothing to do with starting BrokenStone Ministries. Tim and Terri Abel were very musically gifted college students who came out to our recording studio, known as Osh Gosh, to record an album in the late 1970s. Their music ministry was growing. An accountant friend was led to do the paperwork, and BrokenStone Ministries non-profit came into existence. Tim and Terri asked if I would be one of the three on the board of directors. I gladly agreed.

Later Tim and Terri settled down, married, and began serving in a local church, so BrokenStone was no longer needed for them. I was moving out into the mission field as they were moving in, so those who were led to support the not-for-profit ministry I was involved in could do so with their gifts being tax exempt.

Every aspect of BrokenStone Ministries/OFA is based on the declaration that friendship rules! We are all about organism, not organization, relationship, not regulation, individual not institution, encouragement and inspiration, not domination and intimidation. We all about life, not law.

## Friendship Rules

*I know a child, beaten and scorned,*
*Cursed by words since the day she was born.*
*Then she met a friend who began to love her fear away.*
*Now, you can see her smile.*
*She found her way.*
*Friendship Rules, friendship reigns.*
*The power of love cannot be contained.*
*Never mind the foolish ones who criticize, condemn, and complain.*
*Friendship Rules, friendship reigns.*
*What a Friend we have in Jesus.*

## The Freedom of Unfailing Love

*I'm learning to not get upset with someone who is upset.*
*I'm learning to not let this troubled world get the best of me.*
*I'm learning to not get offended by someone else's offense.*
*I'm learning to not straddle the fence.*
*I'm learning to live free.*

*Yes, I'm learning to live "the Freedom of Unfailing Love."*
*Learning to feel the power that flows from above.*

## Learning to Love a Porcupine

*I know there's trouble in store.*
*I know there's much, much more we need to learn about*
*"Living the Freedom of Unfailing Love."*

*The Sermon on the Mount is the key.*
*The Master says to love even your enemy.*
*My worst enemy was in the mirror.*
*It's getting clearer and clearer to see:*
*If I'm to love my neighbor,*
*I must first let the Master love me!*
*Catholics confess; protestants protest; sinners transgress;*
*backsliders regress; strippers undress.*
*This world is in a mess: duress, stress, depressed.*
*Is there any rest, success, progress?*

*The answer comes from above.*
*Don't you think it's time we learn*
*To live the Freedom of Unfailing Love?*

# CHAPTER 2

## Our Beloved Bowie

*D*rug addiction, suicidal depression, and the personal, destructive detour on life's highway began for me when my best friend from Jacksonville, Alabama, Bowie Lueallen, was killed in Vietnam. I'd never known anyone to die before that.

Sgt. Edgar Bowie Lueallen

This impersonal account for the record added terrible insult to our injury:

> **"Edgar Bowie Lueallen, SGT—E5—Army—Regular 101st Airborne Division Length of service: 1 year. His tour began on Dec 18, 1965. Casualty was on Apr 16, 1966 in SOUTH VIETNAM, Hostile, died of wounds, GROUND CASUALTY MULTIPLE FRAGMENTATION WOUNDS Body was recovered."**

Bowie was born and raised on the other side of the tracks, Jacksonville Mill Village. By the time he was six, he could out-cuss a sailor and out-smoke a worn-out '58 Chevy needing a head gasket!

His legs were so short they'd barely reach his waistline. He laughed and referred to himself as "duck footed." He had a dimple in his chin, so he claimed kin to the movie star, Kirk Douglas. He was semi-clumsy, with limited athletic ability. However, he made up for it with guts.

Bowie was more than a friend. He was a brother, a leader, and our guide. Many of us were very foolish, awkward adolescents *"picking fights with thunder storms"* and *"charging into trees."* With caution to the wind, we were wandering around drunk on a bootleg case of Country Club Malt Liquor in a no-man's land at the foot of fool's hill.

Bowie was right by our side but different. He was a caring, sensible, influential young man, more mature than his years. You could push the envelope, but you did not cross the line when Bowie was anywhere around. He looked out for us and protected us from ourselves.

Bowie was considerate, caring, and respectful toward our parents and grandparents, even when the rest of us thought it wasn't cool. Most of us were convinced that we knew it all and that grown-ups were

## Our Beloved Bowie

old-fashioned and knew nothing. Bowie was not at all like that. My elderly grandmother, Momma Dee Dee, who lived with us, was always asking about Bowie and looking forward to his coming by. He was so special to each of us.

Bowie was a bright comet that swiftly passed thru. After his death, we were left puzzled and even haunted as to why he was allowed to walk among us for only such a brief period of time.

Even today, the memories of him don't fade. Over these many years, those of us who knew him have grown to appreciate and love him even more.

Even though Bowie was fun-loving like the rest of us, he still had a way of being brutally honest. He was intolerant of all hypocrisy, yet he still had a way of bringing out the best in each of us.

When I got the call, I was a freshman playing football at Mississippi State University. My mother, unable to choke back the tears, gave me the news, "Bowie's been killed!"

As a violent linebacker, I pretended to be tough, but with that call, I quit lying to myself. I was not a "tough guy." Life quit being fun that day.

Death is so damn final! I felt as though all of mankind had a problem with no solution. There was no working through it. I looked at the overall scoreboard and realized that death wins, and the rest of us lose! No exceptions! I began to see life as nothing more than a setup for betrayal and pain, meaningless hypocrisy.

Macbeth said it well! *"A tale told by an idiot, full of sound and fury, signifying nothing!"*

And I was not about to let anybody get close to me, ever again!

"Why bother to conform? If something feels good, why not do it? We're all going to die anyway!" I became a speedboat, out of control, heading straight for hell, with no rudder!

My thinking became: "Get stoned and stay stoned! Who wants to face a cursed life sober? 'God is love,' you say? 'Our Father, Who art in Heaven?' He may be in Heaven, but my family, friends, and I are here on Earth right now. If there is a Sovereign, All-Powerful God like church folks claim, then I don't like him or them!"

I was angry and afraid. Angry because I lost my best friend and afraid because I did not want to get close to another person and go through another loss, ever again.

I had, in ignorance, looked to Bowie to be my conscience, and Bowie died. Where did that leave me?

Years later, one of the soldiers in his platoon, who was with him when he died, emailed me: "Bob, you knew him as Bowie. We knew him as Sgt. Lueallen. Your friend was truly a courageous American hero who literally gave his own life for us."

He also sent me this picture of Bowie watching out for his platoon. It's the same body posture I saw so many times on the football field in between plays!

**Sgt. Lueallen looking out for his platoon**

After 50 years, I still grieve.

People frequently asked him, "How did you get that unusual name, Bowie?" This was always his reply:

## Chinese Custom

*He said his momma used a Chinese custom*
*When she's lookin' for her boy a name.*
*Throw silverware in the air,*
*Hit the ground and that sound, well, that's your name.*
*Like Ching and Chang, Ding and Dang*
*Them Chinese are all to blame.*
*'Cause when his momma's tablespoon fell in a tub of water,*
*"Bowie" became his name!*

*Aunt Bessie's fried chicken for Bowie and his buddies*
*'Fore school and I reckon*
*I'll never forget*
*How the love made me high.*
*And High School buddies are special*
*And especially Bowie's kind*
*Lord, why are they sometimes so quick to die?"*

## Case Sensitive

*It doesn't seem to matter to God who I am or if I'm crazy!*
*Confused, abused, distressed, depressed*
*And sometimes lazy!*

*The bridges I've burned or the friends who turned on me
Leaving me high and dry!
Good neighbors, good fences,
The truth, the consequences of believing a lie!*

*"Momma, the blood, sweat, and tears are burning my eyes!
Momma, every town down here is full of violence, fear,
    and lies!"
Families dying, children crying, hiding in the corner of
    a room
With no room to move, statistics prove:
The most violent dangerous place today is in the USA
In your mother's womb.
Could it be, the only God I've been able to see
Is powerless and disgraced.
Just another word,
Ought to be spelled with a lowercase "g"!*

*In this rental, mental institution called "Planet Earth"
Who can afford the room and the board?
Somebody tell me,
What is one soul worth?
Aggravation, agitation, frustration, intimidation
From imagination run wild!
Sometimes I feel so alone,
So far from home
Like a motherless child!*

## CHAPTER 3

## Nearly Got Hank Jr. Killed

I've been playing with words and rhymes and writing songs ever since I can remember. I can't help but compose what I am living. After the heartbreak of Bowie's death, my songs became nothing but hopelessness, drinking, wild living, renegade, outlaw, and some, even heresy and blasphemy. No restraints. All caution to the wind—I was trying my best to not give a damn!

A particular event, one of the many drug-induced, toxic-psychosis, bright-idea midnight-rainbow dreams, blew up in our face. It was Saturday, May 13, 1978.

The afternoon before The Talladega Winston 500 Stock Car Race, I rented the Freeman Dirt Short Track across the road from the International Speedway, and produced and promoted the first and last Bama Boogie. It headlined none other than Bocephus himself, Hank Williams Jr.

At the time, Hank lived in Cullman, Alabama, and when he was off the road, I'd hire his band to record in a studio I had built onto our home.

## Learning to Love a Porcupine

Without my wife Patti's consent, being totally inconsiderate of her and our children, I closed in the garage and built a control room attached. Concrete blocks filled with sand sound-proofed it from the rest of the house. It had been designed by acoustic engineers from Birmingham, Alabama, and was state-of-the-art. We called the studio "Osh Gosh," a nickname for the rural community we live in.

Backwoods NE Alabama was filled with good ole' boy, redneck, wannabe singer/songwriters. They were "Conway stole my song" country boys, off key, no rhythm, out to make it big.

They had their cowboy hats, bag of dope, Pabst Blue Ribbon Belt Buckles and boots. With their out-of-tune guitars, they would somehow scrape up enough money to hire Hank's band, pay for studio time, and make a 45-rpm record in a real, legitimate, recording studio.

We could put out the vinyl discs with a big hole in the middle and make good money doin' it. Our plan should not be called good, though. It made a way to keep the self-destruction going. It was suicide-on-the-installment-plan; it took money and catering to the hillbilly wannabes to bring the money in.

The first and last Bama Boogie was a miracle! A miracle that no one was killed! After the disastrous event was over and the dust had settled, Hank stepped down from his bus, looked at me through those sunglasses and said, "Cuz! You nearly got us killed!"

I was obviously a loser, totally embarrassed and ashamed.

"Yeah, I know. Sorry, Hank."

Here's how the disaster happened:

A couple of months before our dream concert, Robert, a weed-smokin' cohort, and I were "kicked back," sitting in the attic over Pee Wee's Pasquale's Pizza and Bar looking out the window down on the

## Nearly Got Hank Jr. Killed

Square in Jacksonville, Alabama, passing a marijuana joint back and forth and brainstorming.

"I'd like to see someone with enough guts to book a heavy metal rock band on the same show with a southern rock band like Hank's," Robert said.

That's all it took. The next day I was on the phone, and the Bama Boogie now was going to include in the all-star line-up none other than the electrifying band known as "Warm," the loudest, hottest, rock group in the Southeast.

I hired another cohort, Billy Bob, who was an out-of-work, drunk, drugged-up country DJ. He said he would take care of the details. I remained stoned in a cannabis cloud, not caring what happened. What turned out to be a major problem was that Billy Bob was in that same "don't-care cloud!"

Show time came! All advance ticket money had been embezzled and spent on drugs. Billy Bob was stoned out of his mind. So was I.

The 100-degree summer heat, no breeze made it miserable. We were about to reap what we had sown: Hell on Earth!

Country-redneck race fans started showing up, already drunk, wanting to hear Hank sing "Cheatin' Heart" and all of his daddy's other hits. And we better have the steel guitar and fiddle plugged in and ready to go.

We overlooked and forgot one minor detail! There was no electricity to the stage! Therefore, the show was delayed for at least two simmering hot, dry, dusty, miserable hours, giving the already hostile, volatile crowd plenty of time to brew!

Ronnie, a high school buddy from years past, just happened to be there. He was a lineman for Alabama Power Company. Without Ronnie and his volunteer helper, my young cousin Lloyd, I probably would have been attacked and possibly killed by the irate fans. What's worse, Ronnie and Lloyd cared, but for obvious reasons, Billy Bob and I didn't!

As the Bama Boogie progressed, sweat-drenched race fans in their NASCAR tank tops, faded jeans, and cowboy boots were getting sunburned, meaner, and wilder with each hot beer and swig of whiskey.

Fights were already breaking out, and there was no security staff! Billy Bob and I never thought of that! The beginning of a mass riot was interrupted by the show finally getting underway.

"Warm" hit the stage with their long, hippie hair and their amps cranked up. In an instant, the mindless mob erupted, bombarding the young rockers with a barrage of whiskey and beer bottles, cursing insults, and literally began running toward the stage to physically beat the young long-haired musicians and tear their equipment apart.

Our savior came not too soon. His name, Merle Kilgore. Merle was, in his own right, a country music legend of sorts. He wrote "Ring of Fire" with June Carter Cash and wrote the famous song, "Wolverton Mountain," and some other country hits. He was best man at John and June's wedding.

Merle had played and sang on the Louisiana Hayride with none other than Elvis. He later went on to become Hank Jr.'s manager, taking his career to superstar status.

Merle had been recording in our studio and had become more than an acquaintance. He was one of the few who later encouraged me in my relationship with Jesus.

Merle was the Bama Boogie Master of Ceremonies, and he skillfully and masterfully distracted the crowd. The Warm band members, all young rockers, fled for their lives.

# Nearly Got Hank Jr. Killed

Merle brought Hank on stage. Hank began singing the crowd's favorite songs, including one about a wooden Indian named "Kawliga." He sang the correct lyrics, but I heard a different meaning of the words, *". . . is it any wonder that his face is red? Bob McLeod, that poor old wooden head!"*

Late that night, when the crowd was gone, I stood there alone. The drugs had worn off. What I saw made me sick. I stared around at the remains of the mess I had made. In front of me was a sea of bent, empty beer cans, broken whiskey bottles, blood here and there, and a few people passed out in the mud. I was financially and emotionally broken and ruined.

A leftover, hungover straggler stumbled up behind me and offered me a hit off his joint. I dropped my head and walked away. I was sick enough to die to the horrible way I had been living.

How I dreaded going home, but there's nowhere else to go when you're broke and broken.

At home, there were two little boys, ages three and five, and a newborn baby girl in need of a daddy. There was a faithful mother and wife who had suffered through nine years of marriage, in need of a Godly husband, not some inconsiderate, self-consumed loser who was pretending to be cool.

In reality, I had been nothing but a fool, a wretched, stubborn, self-centered, self-willed bird insisting he have it his way, repeatedly flying into a plate glass window. I was confused, angry, afraid, sin-sick, and totally exhausted. I had officially arrived at the pig trough mentioned in that Bible story about The Prodigal Son in **Luke, Chapter 15**.

I arrived home. Stumbled thru the back door. The clock was approaching 3 a.m. There, sitting on the sofa in the corner of the den, staring into space, and softly weeping, sat my wife. A dim light from the lamp on the end table cast a faint shadow of a lonely soul, abused by neglect, fearful for her children, and her dreams of a happy home shattered. She didn't even acknowledge my coming in. No insults, no criticism, no complaints—only sobs and a stream of soft tears.

That morning, suffering love held up a mirror to me and allowed me to see clearly, without excuse, the self-centered monster that I'd become. I hated myself!

## So, Help Me God

*The journey's over.*
*My friends are gone for good.*
*Thought they really loved me.*
*I never understood.*
*People take advantage.*
*The damage is done.*
*Unworthy to call you my Father.*
*I don't deserve to be your son.*

*So, Help Me God,*
*Seems I lost my way.*
*So, Help Me God*
*Make it thru another day.*
*I feel so alone,*
*A million miles from home.*

*I can't make it on my own.*
*So, Help Me God*

## Nearly Got Hank Jr. Killed

*I'm not the man that I used to be*
*And I never was.*
*It was a masquerade for me.*
*Now, I must face reality.*
*Holy God,*
*Have mercy on me!*

## CHAPTER 4

## The Night the Old Man Died

Try to put out a fire using gasoline. That's exactly what happens when one tries to treat depression with alcohol! On several occasions, I would find myself sitting alone in a dimly lit room, hopelessly tormented, with a bottle of Wild Turkey 101 Proof Bourbon Whiskey in my left hand and a loaded Ruger LCR 38 Revolver in my right. I'd gently massage my temple with the tip of the barrel musing as to how easy it would be to end my torment! The hopeless depression was so intense, it was like a steamroller rolling over my head! That's the only way I know to describe it.

One-eighth-of-an-inch trigger pull away from exiting this Earth into an eternity that some Bible believers claim is a never-ending, hopeless torment. One eighth of an inch away!

My unexpected 3 a.m. encounter with suffering love—seeing a precious devoted mother and faithful wife left there alone, crying, and knowing that I was the only one to blame came crashing down on me like an avalanche! The evil seeds I had sown had become like boulders, and there was no way to escape!

No excuse. No justification. I knew right then and there, the inconsiderate, self-centered, sinful life I'd been living was over! Never again! I thought the only way there could be to end it was that Ruger pistol in the side-table next to the bed upstairs.

I made it up the stairs, just a few feet away from the side-table, stumbled, and suddenly fell to the floor. Like a man being trapped in a vise, fighting for each breath, becoming progressively physically crippled and paralyzed, I was barely able to reach up, grab the side of the bed, fight and struggle to my knees. All dignity gone! Engulfed in the horrible darkness of Hell itself, a helpless creature falling into an inescapable black hole. The intensity of guilt, condemnation, regret, shame, the horror of self-hatred, were literally consuming me! I was drowning in it! I began crying out into the darkness, into what I thought was nowhere:

*"Lord, Jesus Christ, I've made fun of You, and I've made fun of people who say they know You. You may be a superstitious myth, a crutch for old people who know they're about to die. All I know is I've made such a total mess out of my life! Jesus Christ, if You're real, please HELP me! Please save me! If You're real!"*

Nothing seemed to happen except that I collapsed and passed out on the floor. I never made it to that pistol, so obviously, something did happen. I lived.

The next morning, I awoke to the smell of bacon cooking. Patti was downstairs in the kitchen cooking breakfast for our family. The horror of the night before had passed. The vise had released its grip.

Miracle number two: no hangover. After washing my face and brushing my teeth, I started down the stairs to sincerely apologize and ask for her forgiveness, when our excited little five-year-old son ran up to me and began to pull on my pants leg.

"Daddy, Daddy, come look. You've got to see this! There's an alligator in the tree!"

I smiled and told him, "You're right! I've got to see it."

He pulled me out through the same back door I'd stumbled through only a few hours earlier.

"Look! There it is!"

Imagine that. An alligator disguising himself as a lizard!

I looked up and saw, in wonder, the first blue sky I had ever noticed. A brightly colored butterfly danced a fluttering ballet in mid-air. For the first time in my memory, I truly heard birds singing. I had begun to live, yet I had not experienced even one religious or spiritual thought.

A week later, I bought a modern translation Bible. I had read the Bible before in order to get ammunition to argue with religious people. However, this time it was different. These are the words I remember reading:

**John Chapter 1**: ". . . and the Word was God . . . In him was life, and that life was the light of men. . . . He was in the world, and even though the world was made through him, the world did not recognize him. He came to his own, but his own did not receive him. Yet to those who do receive him, who believe in his name, He gives the right to become children of God."

**John Chapter 3:17**: "He did not come to condemn. He came to save."

After reading those words,

## THE LIGHT OF GOD WHO IS LOVE FLOODED INTO MY SOUL!

I fell on my knees and began to pray and praise Him!

*"Heavenly Father, I see it now. Suffering and death are not your fault. Suffering and death are the consequences of our selfish rebellion against You. I have been judging and condemning and rejecting You, the Innocent One Who is Truth; Who is Mercy; Who is Grace; Who is Love."*

Jesus, by His Spirit, began to reveal His love to me, and I began falling in love with a living Person, the One Who is Who He claims to be, the Way, the Truth, and the Life. The One Who never says, "Shame on you." The One the Holy Bible is all about!

I do not understand how a light works, but I'm not going to sit in the dark until I do. I do not understand how God's love works, but I'm going to let Him love me anyway!

Since that fateful morning when I started to awaken and see God's handiwork, a longing and hunger for His Word was born within me. The Lord Jesus Christ became my dearest Friend Who is always here to inspire, encourage, and even lift me up whenever I fail or fall.

Since that fateful morning, I began to see Jesus as my Counselor, Companion, Provider, Comforter, and Guide, the One Who embodies Eternal Life; the One Who is the **Psalm 23** Shepherd!

I've often been accused of being superstitious, naive, and deceived; of praying to one who does not exist, nothing but a myth. *Call it what you like*! That *"Jesus, if You're real"* prayer at three in the morning took place in 1978.

That's when my wife got a new husband! My children got a new daddy! My cursed life became blessed! *Call it what you like*! I don't need drugs to face life anymore! *Call it what you like*! All I know is that I once was blind, but now I see! *Call it what you like!* I have been so honored to see the Light turn on for so many others with lasting evidence of transformed lives! *Call it what you like!* A myth cannot do that!

The Light turning on for me does not make me any more special or better than anyone else. Jesus is available to "reverse the curse" for anyone who is simply willing for Him to do it His way. Jesus is Emanuel, God with us, all of us.

I am personally convinced that death is a mere shadow, an illusion, and the dead are not dead, even though we can't physically see them.

The songs I was writing changed instantly, and since then, all I write is about Him!

"He lifted me out of a slimy pit, out of the mud and mire; he set my feet on a rock and gave me a firm place to stand. *He put a new song in my mouth, a hymn of praise to our God.* Many will see and fear and put their trust in Him." **Psalm 40:2–3**

## The Night the Old Man Died

*I used to know an old man who was wayward.*
*Born to take advantage of everyone in sight.*
*Evil, mean, and wild.*
*Every thought sick and defiled.*
*Quick to cuss, and he loved to fuss,*
*Go out of his way to fight.*
*Some say they saw him driving my car.*
*Some even claim that he called my wife his own.*
*My children called him Daddy.*
*He even lived in my house*
*But that was before it became a home.*
*I'll lift my voice and thank the Lord that he died.*
*He was last seen on a hill called Calvary.*

*The night Jesus Christ came into my life.*
*His Glorious Spirit was born in me!*

*The Night the Old Man Died.*
*A new child came alive,*
*All because of a cross on a hill called Calvary.*
*The Night the Old Man Died.*
*A new child came alive,*
*When I let Jesus give His Life to me.*

*The Night the Old Man Died*
*He'll never neglect and ignore his children again.*
*His wife will never be left crying at night at home alone again.*
*Now there's one less clown in the downtown bar.*
*One less drunk on the road in a car.*
*He found out who his friends really are.*
*Some abandoned him.*
*The Night the Old Man Died*

## CHAPTER 5
# God Sent an Angel to Turn a Devil Around

She was a beautiful, Gem of the Hills majorette and marching ballerina. She was pure, innocent, naive, predictable, and precious. Working her way through school, she carefully set goals and made plans. Her course of life was right straight down the middle of the beaten path; cautious, committed, playing it safe, preparing for the future.

She became a devoted mother, relishing her kids' Little League, Cub Scouts, and Barbie Dolls. She earned a Master's Degree in Elementary Education, a dedicated schoolteacher, faithful wife, children's Sunday-school teacher, Cub Scout Den Mother; but in spite of all that, she really messed up!

She married an inconsiderate, self-centered, party animal; a reckless, devil-may-care linebacker who was violent enough to win a college scholarship but irresponsible enough to throw it away.

The violence turned within. He flunked out and became an eccentric drunk, pot head, pill-poppin' drifter, poet, and writer of depressing suicide songs.

# Learning to Love a Porcupine

**Patti Brown**
**Jacksonville State University Marching Ballerina**

He was so far off the beaten path that there seemed to be no way back for him, but he didn't seem to care anyway. He figured he'd dug his own grave too deep, hopelessly lost. What did she ever see in him?

Many nights as she would put their children to bed, he would be wasted, hanging out in some old abandoned apartment building or smoke-filled, cheap tavern on Music Row or anywhere else Hank Williams, the miserable genius songwriter who drank himself to death at age 30, was idolized and held up as a role model.

The loser found his identity in the subculture of Woody Guthrie wannabees, passin' around a joint with an old, out-of-tune guitar, singin' *"who's to blame ballads"* until dawn; then passin' out, unconscious, on an old, dingy, mildewed, rotten, linoleum, roach-infested floor.

The beast that the beauty had married was red eyed, chain smoking, coughin', hackin', stumbling around lost in a cannabis cloud of smoke, trying to find his place; a dreamer in an underground-gutter university working on his PhD in insanity, with a specialty in drugs'll kill ya!

He was doing extensive research on how to wreck a life; becoming well qualified to write a book on *How Not to Treat Your Wife*. He became a master of the disaster that comes when the cheap thrills no longer thrill ya!

That self-destructive, self-centered sinner I refer to in the third person was the man I used to be, not who I am today. I became a new creature at 3 a.m. that morning in 1978. **2 Corinthians 5:17** took place within me! The old man died!

It's now so apparent that the years I spent in addiction, self-destruction, depression, and torment were preparing me to offer a lifeline to others, to share the hope I had found with those living in the same, insane nightmare I had come out of.

Patti has remained by my side, riding life's roller coaster together with our Lord since June 14, 1969.

When I recall those dark years and how I'd came so close to destroying myself and missing this blessed, wonderful, joy filled-life, I breathe an eternal sigh of relief, and tears of gratitude continue to fill my eyes.

All because Jesus Christ lives in a precious lady who had every legitimate reason to give up on me.

Today our children call me, not someone else, "Daddy," and our grandchildren lovingly call me "Papa"! I came within one eighth of an inch from missing the greatest blessing life has to offer: A loving family!

I have no bad days! I am so grateful!

"Yes, Jesus, You are the Way, the Truth, and the Life, You are so Real! Thank You, Precious Lord! Because of You, goodness and mercy are following me all the days of my life, and I will dwell in Your house forever!" Glory!

As you will see in subsequent stories, we have been personally, actively involved together in the lives of countless precious souls who have also found hope and a new life. To our Lord Jesus Christ be all the glory!

Maybe Patti didn't mess up so bad after all.

Bob and Patti McLeod 2017

## Suffering Love

*She was all about living*
*I was all about dying.*
*She was all about thanksgiving.*
*Until I left her alone, crying.*
*She was all about purity.*
*I was all about sin.*
*She was all about Little League,*
*Cub Scouts, and Barbie Dolls.*
*I was all about turning within.*

## God Sent an Angel to Turn a Devil Around

*She was sent from Heaven for a soul Earth bound.*
*God sent an angel to turn a devil around.*

*Suffering Love*
*Is how I came to see,*
*It's all about Him Who sent her for me.*
*Suffering Love,*
*Another captive set free.*
*It's all about love, It's all about love, It's all about love*
*I see in the precious wife God's given to me.*

*She didn't have to stay.*
*She could have run away.*
*When the going got tough*
*She endured day by day and continued to pray!*

One more song lyric about dear, precious Patti:

## *She is*

*God in Heaven never crossed my mind*
*When I saw her dance and twirl,*
*Stars in my eyes, butterflies,*
*Staring at the world's most beautiful girl.*
*She was the beauty.*
*I was the beast.*
*Too numb, too dumb to know what to say.*
*Found it hard to believe*

*That she would even offer me*
*Any more than the time of day.*

*My wife, my friend, She is.*
*Mother of our children, She is.*
*Meme to our precious grandkids, She is.*
*She doesn't try to be a vital part of me but, She is.*

*50 years later, I'm still amazed*
*How God in Heaven smiled on me that day!*
*I pray He'll help me hold her gently*
*Because I know that She's His*
*A reflection of His unfailing Love,*
*She is.*

# CHAPTER 6

## My Friend, Ken

The 1964 Jacksonville High School Golden Eagles football season didn't make the record books. Ken Brown, a loudmouthed freshman, was a running back with no helmet or pads. He'd run back and forth and on and off the field with a towel, ice-water bucket, ammonia capsules, and private off-color jokes.

Ken truly brought an extra flare of "behind the scenes" entertainment to the game. He was Dennis the Menace, Don Rickles, and Rich Little all in one.

We tried our best to be serious about the games. Locker-room rules were clear: Keep it quiet. No idle conversations. No horseplay. Concentrate on the game. Conserve energy. Then, in would come Ken, breaking the silence with his impersonation of one of our beloved coaches nicknamed "Rat" and leaving us hyperventilating from laughter.

Ken must have been a secret weapon for the opposing teams. Our dwindling number of fans wondered how we could lose so many games with so much talent!

## Learning to Love a Porcupine

**High school hangout**

In the off-season, Ken was a carhop at Cecil Marbut's Rocket Drive-in just south of town. On weekends, the place would rock and roll. The high school shindig was on: letter sweaters, bobbie socks, Elvis, the Beach Boys, the Beatles, and the Rolling Stones: "Hey, Hey, You, You, Get Off of My Cloud!" Radios blaring.

Kids with car keys! Free at last! Horseplay in overdrive! Fighting for the black, curly cord phone that hung loosely under the homemade sheet-metal stand on a metal pole next to each car and, all at the same time, we'd scream in the order.

"Four double meat Rocket Burgers, fries, three chocolate shakes, two large cokes—no wait—make that onion rings on one of 'em. What'd you say? Make that cheese! Ha Ha. How much? Hang on."

Pockets emptied, along with quarters, nickels, pennies, and wrinkled up dollar bills. Back to phone, "Yeah, we got it. Send it on!"

Twenty minutes later, here comes Ken! Balancing in each hand a worn Teflon car-window tray, he'd burst out backwards from the kitchen through the swinging screen door, headin' for the cars.

# My Friend, Ken

Steaming hot, fried, greasy, southern smell, leaking mustard with ketchup on soggy paper napkins and cardboard containers about to be pounced on by a car full of hungry, inconsiderate vultures.

Mr. Marbut's Friday and Saturday nights had to have been a nightmare for him, juggling orders from a dozen cars that were hiding places for hot, bootleg beer, raging hormones, wild teenagers pretending to be cool, finally free from their parents—or so we hoped.

Adding to the madness of the mindless teenage crowd was Ken, the wild ringmaster leading the circus; runnin', laughin', jiving', jeerin', jugglin', helping himself to the greasy fries and sips on the shakes as he'd run from car to car. Only Ken could have gotten away with that.

Love him or love to hate him, there was no way to get rid of him. I was one of the ones who loved him.

Graduating or simply turning sixteen and dropping out of school changes everything for everybody. Life gets much more serious and complicated. The footloose, fancy-free days of running with like-minded high school buddies, locker-room jokes, and competing for the girls' attention is gone forever.

When I heard that Ken enlisted and headed for Vietnam, I knew the troops over there were in for some entertainment. And they didn't even have to wait for Bob Hope or Red Foxx.

Unlike some of our buddies, Ken made it back. But he was never the same. The horrible carnage and bloodbath of war hit him hard, and he came home with deep personal, emotional damage. Like many other veterans, war knocked all the sanity out of Ken.

He married and became the dad of two children. He even became a preacher, a real zealot for God. Hatcher Avenue Baptist Church definitely had a spark plug in Ken. That was until . . .

## Learning to Love a Porcupine

Ken was so outgoing that he could sell anything: Rocket Burgers, furniture, or Jesus Christ. The furniture store was his headquarters during the week. After hours, the doors closed and locked, out would come the bottle, in would come the drink, out would come the demons.

Too much alcohol puts the conscience to sleep. Imagine Ken Brown without a conscience. It was worse than that. The devil got him, and his family lost him, and so did his church. Ken lost his dignity and his self-respect. A meager, monthly US government disability check became his enabler.

It was 30 years after our carefree high school days that I found Ken holed up in a dilapidated, wrecked house trailer with no electricity because of non-payment. It had an awful stench from an overflowing toilet seldom flushed. With Ken was his fat, fluffy, smelly puppy he'd named "Bear," after his hero, the University of Alabama legendary football coach, Bear Bryant.

Ken's house trailer was like stepping into one of hell's garbage dumpsters. Inside were dog poop and urine, old, open, molded cottage cheese cartons, empty beer cans, and Campbell's soup cans strewn all over the floor, ashes and cigarette butts everywhere. Sitting in the middle of it all, lying back in an old, worn-out armchair was my old high school buddy, Ken.

His face was wrinkled way beyond his years. His skin was like sunburned pork rinds. His nicotine-stained hands trembled. His hair was gray, thin, and receding. A scar on his forehead was the reminder of one of the nights he took a beating when his drunken, smart mouth called for blows. Another drunk beat him in the head with a pool cue, leaving him for dead in a back alley.

I walked in, and my heart broke. I told Ken that I loved him and offered to help him clean up his place. He mumbled some smart remark

## My Friend, Ken

about Crimson Tide Football and fell asleep. I put out his cigarette butt, took the dog Bear outside, and began some straightening and cleaning, a task impossible for one person to finish in a day—or a month, for that matter.

I made a little progress, let Bear back in, went home, threw my smelly clothes into the washer, took a shower, and returned the next day to check on Ken. I took him to meet his appointment with a doctor, and then we went to the health department, the probation officer, and anywhere else he felt he needed to go. We went everywhere but the beer store, that is.

One day with Ken became two, then another and another. Two weeks later, Ken's sister called me and was amazed that Ken had been sober for so long. I was mistakenly too idealistic to believe that, after all these years, the nightmare could miraculously end and that Ken could be a sober new man overnight.

One day I missed seeing him. A week went by. I stopped by his trailer to check on him, and, there he was, the same as before. His check had come in, and he had no trouble getting a ride to the liquor store. Ken had friends who would come by to check on him only at the beginning of the month. Sounds like "love with a hook in," doesn't it?

My wife, Patti, and I were awakened from a deep sleep one night, the phone blaring like a fire alarm. "Uhhhhh, hell-o?"

"Hey, Bob—this is Ken," he said. His tongue thick and speech slurred, he said, "Coach Bear Bryant and me are over here talkin' about the great Bob McLeod, the Golden Eagle Linebacker turned songwriter. We just wanted to call and tell you we love you."

I reacted. "No, you don't, Ken! You love that damn bottle. Don't you ever call here again."

I slammed the phone down but was so infuriated that I stayed wide awake the rest of the night.

## Learning to Love a Porcupine

The nerve, I thought. Why did I ever give that hopeless, inconsiderate drunk my phone munber? He's nothing but a nuisance!

I turned to Patti and apologized.

The next day was Wednesday, the day my friend Mac and I would meet at the gym and work out. Mac was an old college football teammate who was on staff at Jacksonville State University. We'd warm up for our workout by jogging around the track above the gymnasium in the Pete Matthews Coliseum.

It was summer-camp time, and junior high kids from all over the county were waiting for their counselors to arrive at nine to get things started. Most of the kids were crowded near the front door, excited and energetic.

There was a loner, however: a precious little girl, no taller than four-foot-five. She was at the end of the gym, trying her best to throw the large basketball through the hoop.

She didn't seem to mind if anyone was watching. She'd hold the ball in both hands, stoop as low as she could, and, with all the energy she could muster, push upward, the ball falling way short. With amazing tenacity and determination, she'd run for the ball, move back in front of the hoop, and try again and again. As Mac and I would jog by, we started cheering her on.

"Hey, try it again! You can do it," we'd shout as we'd run by.

She began looking over her shoulder for us to come by again. As soon as she'd see us, she'd try again, each time getting closer and closer.

"You can do it! Try it one more time."

Then, to our amazement, the ball swooshed through the net. We began to clap, dance, and cheer.

"We knew you'd make it! Way to go! You're awesome!"

She was beaming!

## My Friend, Ken

About half a lap later, I was deeply convicted. It was if God were saying to me, "Bob, you gave up on Ken, but I didn't. Go tell him he can make it. Try it one more time."

I found Ken at a run-down apartment of one of his unsavory, after-payday cohorts.

He was obviously high, drinking a beer, and runnin' his mouth, as usual!

"Ken," I told him, there, right in front of his buddy. "I gave up on you, but God didn't. Let's try it one more time!"

He and I got down on our knees together and prayed.

As it came to pass, Ken and I tried several more times, with what appeared to be limited success. Only a few years later, Ken died of a massive heart attack, leaving a troubled life of intoxication and turmoil, in and out of jail, in and out of Veteran's Hospitals, vacillating between hope and despair.

Some years earlier, I had recorded a cassette album of ten songs called, *Bug Zapper*. The title song, Ken's favorite, relates to how we humans are drawn into destruction by our lusts like insects are drawn to the light of a Bug Zapper only to get stuck and/or fried!

## *Bug Zapper*

*What one man calls a blessing,*
*Another man calls a sin.*
*Some men run around guessing*
*While other men just pretend.*
*We can all learn a lesson*
*About the wages of sin*

From a bug who sought a blessing
And how the blessing done him in!

Bug Zapper,
Such a beautiful light,
Bug Zapper, shining in the night.
Lures 'um in, sets 'um up, blows their mind
'Till they end up stuck!
A high flyin' bug up and died,
Though he's havin' fun 'til he got fried!
Beware, the Bug Zapper!

We can pretend that sin's not sin,
It's a blessing and not a curse.
Make believe all is well,
When all is gettin' worse!
There's a neon sign over hell
Sayin', "It's fun, come on in."
But the truth is still the truth
And death is still the wages of sin.

## Al K. Hall

Blames his ole' lady.
She ran off with the baby to parts unknown.
She won't answer the phone when he calls.
She's tired of being hurt by Al K. Hall.

## My Friend, Ken

*Al K. Hall was havin' a ball,*
*Thought he had it all until he took the fall.*
*Sits alone in a smoke-filled haze,*
*A month of Sundays since he's bathed or shaved.*
*God-awful stench, his back is against a rotten, roach-*
  *infested wall.*
*Everybody's tired of being hurt by Al K. Hall*

*He took 11 steps and then he fell.*
*Let go of the hope of Heaven*
*Grabbed a hold of Hell.*
*Got to where he wouldn't work,*
*Lost his family, lost his shirt,*
*Turned into a first-class jerk!*
*Wasted, waitin' on a wake-up call.*
*Everybody's tired of being hurt by Al K. Hall*

*Al K. died one day and a new Al Hall came alive.*
*Washed in the blood, filled with love,*
*Born again and baptized.*
*His wife and his child came home.*
*Al's no longer alone with his back to the wall.*
*He heard the wake-up call.*
*Now everyone's praising God, His wife glorifies God.*
*His little girl gets down on her knees at night*
*And thanks Jesus for her daddy,*
*Reverend Al Hall*

# CHAPTER 7

## Can a Hell Raiser Go to Heaven?

The "Bug Zapper" cassette tape album became for Ken like the Lone Ranger's silver bullet, his calling card.

By far, most of the places I have ever gone and shared the songs I've written have been among people who have no money; therefore, there's no charge. I've given away countless numbers of albums over the years.

How can we afford to do that? Good question! Looking back, giving the albums away has probably generated more income than if we'd sold them!

*"Freely receive, freely give,"* remains the motto of BrokenStone Ministries' financial policy. If the funds are not there, then we simply stop spending—no more albums to give away or anything else.

For more than four decades, that has never once happened! The funds continue to flow in, often times from places we thought was nowhere and often times just in time!

The miracle is: we continue to *"be fruitful and multiply"* beyond anything we could expect or think! We read about that in **Ephesians 3:20!**

Before he died, Ken was constantly asking for more Bug Zapper tapes. Wherever he went, he would pass them out, sowing them like seed.

Each of the nude dancers, bartenders, and drunks at dark, out-of-the-way places, like the Fox Trap Club on Saturday nights; the doctors, nurses, and staff at the VA Hospital on his occasional 30-day dry-outs before starting another drinking spree; at the dope houses; even police officers arresting him—wherever Ken went, a Bug Zapper tape would be left in his wake!

**Foxx Trap Gentlemen's Club**

I'd keep Ken supplied, and, occasionally, he'd have me write a $50 post-dated check for him to sign, claiming the money would be there when his government check would come in. Most of the time he would spend it before the check came through.

The last check he had me write for him to sign was a week before his death. After his funeral, I stopped by my mailbox, and there was the returned check from the bank: non-sufficient funds! Ken's last check bounced, and it was to me! How's that for financial planning? To this day, I can almost see him laughing!

Ken was serving weekends in the Oxford City Jail for a DUI and driving without a license conviction. The jail was really his home base. He was a stray during the week, sleeping in abandoned junk

## Can a Hell Raiser Go to Heaven?

cars, under trees, an occasional night on the ragged sofa of a cohort from the toxic subculture who was too obsessed with drugs to be embarrassed by him.

At the jail, he could get a hot shower, wash his clothes, and eat regularly; so, when the judge ordered him to do weekends in jail, it was like throwing Uncle Remus' Br'er Rabbit into the briar patch!

A year before his arrest, Ken suffered a stroke, and his speech was difficult to understand, especially when he was drinking.

One Saturday afternoon, he called me from the jail. I could understand him, so I knew he was sober.

All he said was, "Bob, I love Jesus, and I love you!"

"I love you too, Ken."

"Listen to me!" he said, "I love Jesus, and I love you!"

And then, without further conversation, he hung up the phone. An hour later, while washing his clothes, Ken had a massive heart attack and died.

His sister Geraldine called and asked if I would share some special words at Ken's funeral.

"Of course," I replied, trying to hide my immediate since of dread.

How do you eulogize someone whose life appears to have been so tragic? What comfort can there possibly be for the grown children who had been so embarrassed and hurt or the ex-wives who may dare to show up?

What about the subculture of addicts who were sure to come? Do you tell them that it's okay to continue to live a drunken, destructive, wasted life and continue to hurt the people who love them? And if you read from the Good Book, in good conscience, can you ignore passages like **Galatians 5:19**, where we're told that drunks will not inherit the Kingdom of God?

## Learning to Love a Porcupine

When Friday afternoon at 2:30 p.m. rolled around, K.L. Brown's Funeral Home Chapel was overflowing, standing room only. In the parking lot were new slick, polished Cadillacs next to worn-out, rusted, barely-runnin' clunkers with jumper cables lying where the back seat use to be.

From dignitaries to derelicts, Ken's life had deeply touched this community. Everyone loved him, even those who had hated him or feared him!

And I had the honor of sharing publicly my own love for this colorful character and, in particular, his last phone call from the jail. I suspect he knew that, with that call, he was his giving me instructions for his own funeral!

The night before I was to speak, while praying, contemplating, and preparing, I received a revelation that has been a constant reminder for me, especially during the many funerals where I've been called upon to share since.

*"God did not check with me when He created the universe, and He doesn't check with me as to who is in Heaven and who is not!"*

I'm not here to judge another's soul. I'm here simply to be available to God's Spirit that He might bring comfort and hope to those who remain. Only His Spirit can do that. I am nothing. He is everything!

God put His love in my heart for porcupines, ragamuffins, and outcasts. One of them was named Ken, and I was honored to share a part of life's journey with him.

As the funeral service got underway, I shared with the congregation that I knew Ken loved me.

"He told me enough times over the phone in the middle of the night!" I said jokingly.

Many in the audience laughed, and I realized that Ken had been late-night calling them, too!

## Can a Hell Raiser Go to Heaven?

After the chapel service, I rode with K.L., the owner of the funeral home, in his hearse, which carried Ken's remains to the White's Gap Baptist Church Cemetery. We continued the service at the graveside.

K.L began to laugh and told me of one of his eventful late-night Ken calls:

"K.L. you got any false teeth in that desk drawer of yours?"

K.L., half asleep, replied, "What?"

"Yeah, I got drunk and lost my teeth. You don't bury them perfectly good teeth do ya? Do you have some extras?"

"Yes, Ken, I do bury them, and no, I don't have any. Goodbye."

"Shame on you, K.L., but thanks anyway! Roll Tight, 'uh Tide!"

Alone, driving home from Ken's funeral service, I was reflecting on his life, the trail of broken relationships, the heartbreak, the loved ones who, admit it or not, are probably relieved that he's gone.

I was so heartbroken, realizing that there's so many like Ken around us and that the nightmare is escalating. Who among us, young and old alike, has not been outrageously violated and victimized by this demon called addiction?

## Hand Grenades and Horseshoes

*Reverend Goodman was a good man.*
*Never smoked or drank alcohol.*
*Preached every Sunday and that's not all.*
*Ten Commandments kept in his front yard.*
*"I love Jesus" sticker on the bumper of his car.*
*He didn't think it so bad, the lustful thought that he had.*
*Reverend Doctor I.M. Goodman died in his sleep last week.*

## Learning to Love a Porcupine

*He was remembered by the members*
*Of his high-steepled church on Main Street.*
*Honored and acclaimed, a new plaque bears his name,*
*Outstanding citizen from our outstanding city,*
*But it's really such a pity!*
*Reality found the good reverend one lustful thought away*
*From God's perfect Heaven!*

*Getting close just might do*
*With hand grenades and horseshoes*
*But almost making it to Heaven*
*Is to make it to where you don't want to go!*
*Heaven is a perfect place, and it's only by God's Grace*
*Can a sinner man find an open door!*
*Getting close just might do*
*With hand grenades and horseshoes!*

*Billy Joe Wildman was a wild man!*
*Hooked on drugs and alcohol.*
*Raising Hell every night and that's not all.*
*He killed a guy, DUI, stolen car.*
*Head down, handcuffs, doing life behind bars!*
*Confessed he'd been so bad.*
*Cried out for mercy, broken and sad.*
*Billy Joe Wildman died,*
*A number, not a name, in a lonely prison cell.*
*The state cremated his remains.*
*Despised and ignored,*
*His mother could not afford*

## Can a Hell Raiser Go to Heaven?

*A respectable church with a respectable reverend.*
*But Billy Joe was washed clean by the Blood of the Lamb!*
*Safe in the arms of I Am,*
*And welcomed into God's perfect Heaven!*

*There's some good in everyone.*
*There's some bad as well.*
*None of us are good enough for Heaven.*
*All of us are bad enough for Hell.*

*What can wash away my sin? Nothing but the Blood of Jesus!*
*What can make me whole again? Nothing but the Blood*
  *of Jesus!*
*Oh, precious is that flow that makes me white as snow.*
*No other fount I know, Nothing but the Blood of Jesus.*

# CHAPTER 8

## Dignitaries and Derelicts

During that drive home after Ken's funeral, I was reflecting on the overflow crowd of people from so many different walks of life, people who had gathered together to pay their respects and honor Adrian Kenneth Brown, an eccentric alcoholic, comedian, social outcast.

There we were: for a brief moment, on the same page, on the same stage, masks off.

There we were: helplessly being exposed as to who we really are, not who we, in all of our deception and hypocrisy, had been pretending to be. Our guards were down, each and every one of us, trapped in the undeniable, gut-wrenching, paradox of real-life drama and comedy, tears and laughter, life and death.

There we were: a cross-section of social classes, a coming together that was seldom, if ever seen. Some red, some yellow, some black, some white yet all frail, fragile, frightened, vulnerable human beings.

For a brief moment, mutual love for a fallen friend had united us. Ken, just being Ken, was the unlikely character who'd brought this unlikely group together.

There we were: three-piece suits and ties; faded, frayed, worn-out jeans; even tank tops, flip flops, spit-shined shoes, and everything in between! I didn't notice anybody barefooted, but I'm sure they were there.

Some of us were obviously well-to-do, successful, and reputable pillars of the community. College professors, an assortment of elected officials, and even the mayor himself took time from his busy schedule to be there.

There was another group of self-conscious souls, congregating in the back corner of the chapel, obviously drug users, alcoholics, and addicts who would seldom be seen in a church environment like this; the unmistakable, heartbreaking, persona of souls trapped in an inescapable cage of an addict's horror!

Some of them were skinny as skeletons covered in faded tattoos; weathered, wrinkled, scarred faces, wearing long sleeves on a short-sleeve day obviously to hide the needle marks. Their troubled lives being destroyed, they were living in the hopeless heartache of poverty and self-destruction, just as Ken had done!

Seeing Ken's diverse mixture of loved ones made it obvious: Ken's life was a microcosm of the entire human race. Not only that, but also an amplified mirror reflecting, revealing, and exposing the heart of each of us. Now, it's getting profoundly, painfully personal!

Ken did not land on Earth from another planet! He, like every other demonized addict and criminal, is a product of the human race!

Who among us is not inclined toward selfishness and inconsideration of others? Who among us is not addicted to something or someone?

Mark Twain put it this way: "Everyone is like the moon and has a dark side."

Though it may be difficult to admit, we cannot deny that human beings are obviously, by nature, self-centered, self-destructive addicts—sinners just like Ken! We destroy ourselves and each other as we trash and destroy our planet!

Some are more pleasant and respectable than others and put on a better show, but each and every one of us is: flawed! Ken was simply a "human being *being* a human being!" So am I. So are you!

And though we keep pretending and trying, we're not doing a very good job of fixing ourselves. The self-destruction not only continues but escalates.

By looking at the life of Ken, we can not only gain a better understanding of the plight and dysfunction of the human family but also find hope that transforms and practical, powerful, ways to share that hope with others.

## Have You Seen Jesus?

*They called Jesse a no-count colored man.*
*He lived in a shack on the outskirts of town.*
*The city council was considering*
*Tearing that embarrassing eyesore down.*
*One morning during rush hour,*
*You know how children are,*
*A little girl got away from her mommy,*
*Dashed out in front of a speeding car.*
*Jesse got there just in time*

*To push the child out of harm's way.*
*That so-called no-'count colored man*
*Gave his life saving*
*The mayor's daughter that day.*
*Have you seen Jesus?*
*He's a black man!*

*Jesus is a black man*
*And as a white man He has been seen.*
*Jesus is black, Jesus is white*
*And everything in between.*
*Have you seen Jesus?*
*He's a black man.*

*Bowie's white and seventeen.*
*He joined the Army Corps.*
*Found himself fighting in Viet Nam,*
*In that unholy war.*
*Surrounded by the enemy,*
*His black friend was saved*
*When Bowie threw himself*
*On a detonating hand grenade.*
*Have you seen Jesus?*
*He's a white man!*

*That was Him under a veil*
*Crying in Afghanistan.*
*He's a father, He's a mother, He's a child.*
*He's a woman, and He's a man.*

## Dignitaries and Derelicts

*You can find Him behind prison bars,*
*Sometimes under a steeple.*
*You can find Him anywhere you are,*
*Living and loving thru all kinds of people,*
*Precious people.*
*Have you seen Jesus?*

# CHAPTER 9
## The Affection/Rejection Principle

Just like Ken, the deepest need and motivating factor of every human being is the need for *affection*, therefore, the deepest pain is the pain of *rejection*. It comes from: "*being a human being*!"

The word "affection" carries with it the connotation of physical touching and, as the dictionary defines it, "a gentle feeling of fondness or liking."

Synonyms include love, endearment, care, friendliness, intimacy, attentiveness.

Affection provides one with dignity, significance, encouragement, purpose, inspiration, and hope. Again, affection is every human being's deepest need.

Scientific research confirms that touch can ease pain, lift depression, and, possibly, even increase the odds that a sports team will win.

But touch is even more vital than this: babies who are not held and cuddled and hugged enough might literally stop growing, and, if the situation lasts long enough, even if they are receiving proper nutrition, could even die.

Our friend and ministry partner, Vic Jackopson, was discarded as a child and recalls that, at the age of four, he was for the first time embraced, cuddled, and hugged by a staff lady at the orphanage where he'd been sent. Even though it's been more than 60 years ago, he still recalls that moment with emotion, as if it had been yesterday: "It felt soooo gooood!"

Since affection is one's deepest need, rejection carries with it the most agonizing, deepest pain. It's the frantic self-effort to escape this pain that leads to chemical dependence and addiction. *Therefore, the root cause of addiction is* REJECTION!

There is no way, in this life, on this planet, to escape being rejected. Here are a few examples:

Betrayed by a loved one. This often happens to a child given up for adoption, an unfaithful spouse, an unpaid bill you co-signed, etc. REJECTION!

It may be being born into a home where there's a crossfire of angry, condemning words. Many times, I've heard people say they were told repeated times by a parent, "I wish you'd never been born! You'll never amount to anything!" REJECTION!

It may be being sexually molested, even as a child, bullied on the playground, being embarrassed publicly. REJECTION!

It may be not being accepted by the "in crowd" at school—not making the elite "who's who." It may be when your family can't afford the fees for you to play sports or join the band. You have trouble learning to read, and they call you "slow." You drop out subconsciously convinced you're a failure! REJECTION!

You have to work like a slave and pinch pennies to survive while others pass you by in new cars on their way to the beach. REJECTION!

Your family can't afford to have your teeth fixed, and, whether it's true or not, you feel like others are making fun of you. REJECTION!

## The Affection/Rejection Principle

It may be your physical appearance. Comparing yourself to the celebrity cosmetically made-over beauty queens and kings, you judge yourself as being too tall, too short, too fat, too skinny, big nose, flat feet, bowed legs, or big ears! You think you're ugly! REJECTION!

It may be having everything given to you. Being so spoiled, while the message is subtly being programmed into your subconscious mind, *"You aren't capable of accomplishing anything. Someone else has to do it for you!"* The selfish, spoiled brat with an entitlement mentality caused by: REJECTION!

It may be someone with a Bible and a tract telling you that you will go to hell if you don't believe like they do, and you don't! REJECTION!

It may be seeing everyone so excited and proud of the winning team, and you're the one whose team tried so hard but lost! You feel like a loser! REJECTION!

Your child is confined to a wheelchair. He can't run and play like the other children. He will never walk unless there's a miracle. You borrow money you can't afford to pay back, just to get him to a celebrity Christian healer coming to a major town near you.

You make it! You feel the energy of the crowd! You and the people in your church are believing God for your child's healing! You "sow your seed," putting borrowed money in the collection plate!

The invalid in the wheelchair next to you gets touched by the celebrity, gets up, and dances across the stage, in front of the TV cameras and microphones. The crowd goes wild.

You try to smile and congratulate the one who is healed, but you can't! You are devastated! You have to go home now with nothing but more debt and a broken child God could have healed but didn't!

Now, you feel that even God Himself has rejected you and your child! REJECTION!

And PTSD, post-traumatic stress disorder. Being right in the middle of human beings torturing and savagely killing each other! Seeing a best friend's bloody body parts ripped off and slung across the battlefield! The horror of war too horrible to even document! REJECTION!

And then, there's the dreaded inevitable. The worst rejection anyone can ever experience is the death of a loved one! The one you have grown so close to—the one you love, need, cherish and feel so blessed to be with—suddenly disappears! Oftentimes, without prior notice! You will never hug them again. You will never see them again. There's nothing but an empty, vacant, void, sterile "blank" where life and love used to be, and the "blank" won't go away. A part of you also dies! Can there be any greater REJECTION than that?

*Insulted and assaulted by fear of life's fatal scheme, the fear that what we hold dear will be taken away and it is one day! What can it mean? REJECTION!*

What is the symptom, the evidence of a rejected soul? It's self-centeredness! The human is selfishly trying to get his or her deepest need met, the need for affection!

Self-centeredness obviously tries to control, possess, manipulate, and use others. Self-centeredness whines, complains, scoffs, scorns, shifts blame, pouts, and oftentimes explodes in anger when "I don't get MY way!" All because one's deepest need—the need for affection—is not being met. REJECTION!

Self-destructive addiction (whether socially acceptable or unacceptable) is the eventual consequence of self-centeredness caused by REJECTION.

When I'm offered a way to alter my brain chemistry that gives ME the same feeling affection gives ME, for a moment, even though artificial, I am able to relieve the horrible pain and heartbreak rejection causes.

## The Affection/Rejection Principle

Why not go for it? Especially when I'm in a social group of rejected, desperate souls in the same predicament, doing the same thing.

The artificial high also helps one not to think about the horrible consequences and intensified rejection that's sure to follow when the artificial stimulation wears off.

**Rejection ➡ Self-centeredness ➡ Addiction**

Demonic dominoes: Rejected people reject people, who reject other people. Toxic poison flowing thru the veins of humanity. "Human beings *being* human beings!"

Freedom comes from a personal revelation of affection, an affection that has nothing to do with one's behavior. Unfailing, no hook in it, forgiving, never ending, LOVE demonstrated by the innocent Creator God/Man on a cross more than 2000 years ago is where one's deepest need is met!

That Creator God/Man loves each of us with a passionate affection, so much so that He went thru the torment of hell itself in order to let each of us know!

Not always but oftentimes, rejected, lonely, tormented, self-centered souls make a sterile religion out of Him; that's not Him at all. It's nothing more than another way that rejection-driven tribal leaders control and manipulate others in building their own kingdom that is destined to fall, using the Bible out of context to do it.

*Called "Reverend," I was serving only myself but didn't even know it. Everything I'd do, I'd advertise and try to promote it. Always looking for a pat on the back or hear someone say, "Well done." Trying to convince myself and everyone else that I was one of God's chosen ones!* Manipulating and exploiting hurting people for my own self-centered agenda.

*"The sheep are slowly led to slaughter.*
*Look at the admiration in their eyes.*
*They even sacrifice their sons and daughters*
*Because it's not Jesus,*
*It's the preacher that they idolize.*
*Christianity is the disguise!"*

We can name a tree stump, "Jesus" and bow to it three times a week calling ourselves "Christian." But instead of a tree stump, it's just another religious system with no more power to heal and transform than that dead tree stump! Simply put, another gathering where rejected souls who claim to love each other but can't get along.

*"They sing about amazing grace and*
*How they've been made right.*
*The next thing you know, the First Church of Love's Done broke out in a fight! Uh oh!"*

Ever wonder why there are so many so-called "Bible-believing" churches so close to each other? And the longer we live, the more new ones we see springing up.

*Every street corner has a church, and every church sings a different tune. Some say Jesus just arrived. Others say He's coming soon. Some'll drag you in. Some'll kick you out. Seems self-righteous and absurd. So many disagree yet claim authority in the same Bible, agreeing that it's God's Word!"*

In the midst of all the counterfeits and religious wars, how can we find the real Savior? The One who created us and has simply come to save us from ourselves and heal us. Who is He, really?

# The Affection/Rejection Principle

He can be likened to a mom and dad who comes early to the Tee-ball game to encourage and cheer for their little son Bobby, who's all dressed up and ready to play his first game!

Bobby is so nervous, self-conscious, trying his best to be a winner and make his mom and dad proud. He keeps looking over his shoulder at his parents as they keep shouting his name, cheering for him and his team!

It's Bobby's turn to bat. His little heart pounding, he steps up to the Tee. Swinging with all his might, he keeps missing the ball and knocking down the Tee! The umpire patiently sets it back up, until, on the fourth swing, Bobby finally hits the ball!

Giving it all he's got, his little, short legs moving in slow motion, he stumbles and clumsily takes off toward third base!

Mom and dad come to their feet! Not to condemn him! No! Ridicule or belittle him? Never! They are encouraging him to turn and go in the right direction! *(Isn't that what repentance is? Changing directions?)*

Bobby can't help it! He's just a kid! Bobby is you and me! We are so awkward with life! Mom and Dad understand that Bobby is just a human being *being* a human being.

The real Heavenly Father understands, and He affectionately loves each of us, even when we blow it! He's here to help us learn to run to first base—not to reject us for our missteps!

AFFECTION! AFFECTION! AFFECTION! That's God's heart toward you and me! And, as we mature, it becomes our heart toward each other.

No one will ever experience the intensity and depth of suffering and pain as when our Lord identified with us, took upon Himself the full impact of our REJECTION as He died in bloody agony! But that's not all!

"Up from the grave He arose!" He is alive here and now to affectionately encourage and inspire each of us!

His one commandment (not ten) is to love (demonstrated affection, not rejection), **John 15:12**. And the "how to" is always **1 John 4:19.** "We love because He first loved us!"

**Affection** → **Selflessness** → **Freedom**

Almost always, an individual awakens to this reality by being in an environment and social group where "Love on God's terms" (affection) is demonstrated and lived out. This is the Christ-centered family environment.

Hurting people don't care how much we know until they know how much we care

## Let 'um Know That We're Loved

*The war rages on, violence in our homes.*
*Trouble won't leave us alone.*
*It's all we've ever known.*
*Why are we so afraid?*
*Why are we so depraved?*
*Why are we so frustrated and hated*
*From the cradle to the grave?*
*Because:*

*We don't know that we're loved.*
*We don't know that we're loved*
*Or else we wouldn't be so hostile to each other,*
*Or else we would try so hard to impress each other,*

## The Affection/Rejection Principle

*Or else we wouldn't be so indifferent to each other,*
*We don't know that we're loved.*

*So many children underprivileged.*
*We see them everywhere.*
*Affluent cities, third-world villages,*
*Where the devil doesn't care.*
*A wealthy man commits suicide.*
*A poor man does the same.*
*Middle class struggle to survive.*
*Pass the buck and shift the blame because:*
*We don't know that we're loved.*

*On a hill far away stood an old rugged cross,*
*The emblem of suffering and shame.*
*Was on that old cross*
*The dearest and best*
*for a world of lost sinners was slain!*

*Let 'um Know That We're Loved.*
*Let 'um Know That We're Loved.*
*Give the least of them a helping hand.*
*Let 'um Know That We're Loved.*
*In Jesus' Name we can*
*Let 'um Know That We're Loved.*

## CHAPTER 10

## The Nances Creek Detour

We are so fortunate to live in such a beautiful part of the world. The foothills of the Appalachian Mountain chain provide scenic backroads ideal for leisurely, relaxing drives, allowing one the opportunity to reflect, meditate, and pray, simply sort things out.

At the time of Ken's funeral, I was serving as pastor of Nances Creek Baptist Church, a little country fellowship in rural Calhoun County founded in 1865. Nances Creek is about 17 miles from our home on the other side of the county, so I knew every little scenic nature trail road to and from.

Except for the comfortable ride of a late-model car, it's like going back in time. Nances Creek and the surrounding countryside and mountain range are beautifully *"behind the times."*

Since there was so little traffic, I could drive as slow as I liked. With phone and radio off, windows rolled down, I could relax and bask in the beauty of God's surrounding creation. It was during these scenic, leisurely drives that on occasion I would become aware of the inspiring, unmistakable, still, small voice of our Lord.

Leaving Ken's funeral, I took a detour, the long way home through Nances Creek. Autumn in rural Alabama is like a breathtaking glimpse of Heaven.

Driving through the beautiful, living landscape, I was reminded of these lines from Elizabeth Barrett Browning's poem "Aurora Leigh":

> *"Earth is crammed with heaven,*
> *And every common bush afire with God;*
> *But only he who sees, takes off his shoes,*
> *The rest sit round it and pluck blackberries."*

I pulled over for a moment, took off my shoes, and then resumed the drive—awestruck by the Heavenly beauty around me. Not only was I beginning to see. I was also beginning to hear Him.

Memories began to gently unfold in my mind as I was reminded of these lines from a Mac Davis song, recorded by Elvis in 1971, "Memories":

> *"Quiet thoughts come floating down*
> *And settle softly to the ground*
> *Like golden Autumn leaves around my feet.*
> *I touch them and they burst apart*
> *With Sweet Memories, Sweet Memories."*

I began to remember Lisa. Years ago, I received a call from her. She was a mother of four, a homeless vagrant, strung out on crystal meth, lost and terrified, trapped! No apparent way out! The Department of Human Resources had taken her children and placed them in foster care. Lisa hated herself. She was a homeless mother grieving and longing for her children.

## The Nances Creek Detour

Patti suggested taking her in. I was all for it. To make room, I hung two bed sheets in the entrance ways to our little dining room for privacy. It became Lisa's bedroom. She became like a daughter to us.

After letting her sleep for several days, Patti took her to get some clothes and get her hair done. I took her to see our dentist friend, who pulled a bad tooth. Lisa began to heal. She helped around the house, and, two weeks later, she began working as a waitress at a nearby Waffle House.

After Lisa had been with us for several weeks, I received an anonymous hate call. The party on the other end was cursing Lisa and telling me what a worthless tramp she was.

"She's pregnant again! Ask the bitch about that!" Then the caller abruptly hung up!

I didn't tell Lisa about the call. I simply asked her if she was pregnant. She dropped her head in shame, nodded, and began sobbing.

"Do you know who the baby's dad is?"

"No sir. It's one of three people."

"Lisa, why would a beautiful, intelligent, gifted young lady let men use you like you're a restroom?"

With her head still down in shame, she whispered, "Acceptance."

Lisa gave birth to Timmy, another little boy. In time, she forgave herself and all the many who had used and abused her. After she was healed, she was reunited with her children, who are now all grown, living productive, healthy lives making their momma and family proud!

With Lisa, Patti and I began to see how life-transforming it can be when one is surrounded by people who really care enough to provide a home and place of genuine affection. A place of "hugs" not "drugs." No hidden agendas. Love with no "hook" in it.

Also as I drove, I began to remember Margaret, a heroin addict. Years earlier, I drove her to a Tupelo women's rehab. We kept her son, little four-year-old Daniel, until we were able to find and take him to his grandparents, who were worried sick about him.

After introducing Margaret to the rehab director, I drove home. A few minutes after I left, Margaret hit the director with a chair, smashed out windows, and ran away. We never heard from her again.

With Margaret, Patti and I began to realize that not everyone is ready for help. Our mission is not to "fix" someone—we will worry and be left disappointed if they don't cooperate, and we will be cursed and tormented, and will eventually die of a broken heart.

Our mission is to simply listen and obey our Lord, maintaining our own joy and peace. He's the Savior, not us! We can never lead someone to freedom if we are in bondage to their bondage. We must learn to live with a holy indifference and love each and every one enough to let go.

There were others Patti and I took in. I could tell story after story of what appeared to be successes and failures, but that's not even relevant. Pleasing our Lord is all that matters. We are learning to rest in the fact that, no matter how it appears, love never, ever fails.

We never even considered that our taking people in was a ministry and never even thought to consider why we were doing it. Patti and I are simply two people God brought together who share a mutual affection and appreciation for Him and for each other. That just has a natural way of overflowing.

On the detour home from Ken's funeral, I somehow realized that it was time to do more. I sensed our Lord wanted us to start a home separate from ours so that He could offer a lifeline to more precious souls in crisis.

Our Lord's parable of the Prodigal Son in **Luke 15** is where I, like so many others, have read our own personal story! The self-willed,

## The Nances Creek Detour

self-centered son in that story got to experience where the road of selfish rebellion always leads: the place of desperation and humiliation, homeless, helpless, hungry, broke, and alone!

The son arrived at the end of himself. The only option at this point, other than suicide, was to return home, confess his sin, ask his father for forgiveness, promise to do right from then on, humble himself and ask his father for permission to move in with the servants and to give him a job. So, that's what he did. He turned and headed home humiliated, putting his self-centered contingency plan into action.

What he sees next totally surprises him. He sees his Father running toward him, rejoicing, grateful, full of affection, welcoming him home with the royal robe and signet ring, wrapping his arms around his son!

We never hear his self-centered contingency plan again! The son doesn't have to do right or prove himself. There you have it! Selfishness dies in "'Our Father's Arms!" *Affection evaporates rejection!*

I realized that our home for prodigal sons was to be called "Our Father's Arms," a place of affection, not rejection, a home where relationship rules, not regulation, love, not law!

And then came the mandate that *we were never to advertise or attempt to raise money in any way.* I did not understand!

"Heavenly Father," I prayed, "You know we have our own bills to pay. How can we possibly build a ministry and operate without fundraising?"

The simple reply? *"You'll see."*

That was 1996. The miracles have been multiplying ever since. When our Almighty Heavenly Father gives the vision, He also gives the provision. When He guides, He also provides. Only our Lord Jesus Christ can receive the glory!

## It Finally Dawned on Me

*I see the sun*
*Peeking thru the mountain peaks.*
*I begin to listen.*
*He begins to speak.*
*My life comes alive*
*As the birds begin to sing.*
*The night has passed, the day is here at last.*
*It Finally Dawned on Me*

*It Finally Dawned on Me*
*It Finally Dawned on Me*
*The darkness of night introduces the light.*
*It Finally Dawned on Me*

*For a butterfly to fly,*
*A caterpillar must die.*
*When there's no more room in the cocoon,*
*Thru the strain and the pain, she comes alive.*
*So, it is with you. So, it is with me.*
*It's more than worth the pain of birth*
*For the child to be free.*
*It Finally Dawned on Me.*

# CHAPTER 11

## Heart Bigger Than Head!

"You could build a new house for less than it would cost to repair it. I suggest that you tear it down and start over," Dan said.

I believed Dan. He was an experienced builder and successful businessman, so he obviously knew what he was talking about.

Sam was another friend I met when he was a tormented alcoholic of many years. Thanks to a mental hospital, Prozac, and AA meetings, he had been sober for three years.

Just a few days after Ken's funeral and the Nances Creek Detour, Sam showed up at my home office unannounced. He had no idea that the Lord was leading us to begin OFA in a home other than our own.

"My recovery is in helping other people recover," he said. "I got this old house that I moved out in a pasture. It probably ain't worth fixin', but if your ministry wants to fix it up and take people in, I'll lease it to you for a dollar a year for five years."

I told him, "Thanks Sam, but no thanks."

Surely God would not have Sam to be our landlord! Would He?

The house where OFA began

Sam came back the next day, persistent. "I sure wish you'd reconsider leasing that house."

I did reconsider and told him, "Look Sam, if you've got any expectations, then we're not interested. God may want that house to grow up in weeds just to work patience in you!

Why did you go to the trouble and expense of moving it out there in that pasture anyway?"

"Before my family fell apart, that's where we lived. I lost it in the divorce. Just couldn't stand to see a construction company come through and tear it down, so I bought it back for practically nothin' and moved it out there in my cow pasture. Didn't have nowhere else to put it. Too many memories. I'm too damn sentimental, I guess. I know it ain't worth nothin'. Well, why not, okay, no expectations."

I handed him a five-dollar bill, we signed the lease, and I mostly forgot about it, that is, until a week or so later, I started getting calls from strangers who had somehow heard about it, volunteering to help.

Dan and Brenda Kay were friends who had come out of addiction and prison and had experience in starting residential ministries. They

## Heart Bigger Than Head!

told me that they were being led to move in and be resident directors. Rather than renew their apartment lease for another year in another city, they decided to pack up, come on over, and live with friends nearby until the house was ready.

Dan and Brenda Kay's offer was my confirmation that OFA was to begin, and it was to be in an unlikely, unattractive, unimpressive place: an old dilapidated, rat, roach, and reptile-infested, good-for-nothin' house and yes, with Sam as our landlord!

I stopped being surprised when I realized that our Lord typically chooses unlikely, unattractive, unimpressive places to birth His Kingdom into the Earth. It started 2000 years ago in a smelly manger in Bethlehem.

Now, in our little-bitty world, out in the middle of nowhere, it was happening again! And though no one seemed impressed, it didn't matter. God Almighty was allowing us to take part in His great redemptive plan! Now, that is much more than worth dying for!

I thought that my part was to help get the house livable and assist Dan and Brenda Kay in any way I could, but they would be the ones responsible for the details and day-to-day operation.

Dan and Brenda Kay would take care of the residents and their needs, not only room and board but also the enormous emotional baggage and risk each of them would bring with them. Dan and Brenda Kay would take care of all that, certainly not me! God tricked me!

I was, at that time, working out of our home as a medical recruiter. My one-horse-show business was called McLeod Medical, and I was the one horse.

No secretary. No bookkeeper. No janitor. Just me, a small, worn, wooden desk, filing cabinet, and a telephone with a cord on it! No cell phones yet, so I had to stay within running distance in case it rang!

Most of my competitors were operating out of impressive, plush offices in major cities, even wearing coats and ties to work. High overhead and greed made some of them aggressive sharks, investing thousands in advertising, cutting corporate deals, and, oftentimes, using whatever means necessary to bully us little guys out of business.

I'd be "dialing for dollars," sitting there sometimes in my pajamas in what used to be the control room of Osh Gosh Recording Studio, built on to our home. We lived and I operated our business about two cow pastures away from Possum Trot Road, where you could still find the remains of several moonshine stills hidden in the woods. (Our ancestors struggled to make a livin', too.)

I would simply purchase mailing lists from licensing boards, send out postcards advertising jobs, buy ads in trade publications, make cold calls, and wade thru all kinds of rejection just to find someone who would have a job opening or need a job and be kind enough to listen and let me help them.

Oftentimes, I would gladly give the candidate a good part of my fee if they needed it. We'd call it a "sign-on bonus."

Now, how dumb was that when it looked like I was close to being broke most of the time! It's that *"Heart Bigger Than Head"* scary, dreadful thing I was born with!

I felt so out of place recruitung, but for our livelihood, I felt like I had to do it, so I stayed prayed up, of good cheer, and kept doing it! I met some precious lifelong friends during that season who were later to become supporters of OFA. It was feast or famine but certain famine if I didn't put in the hours.

The contingency fee I'd sometimes get paid for placing a doctor, physical therapist, or other medical professional usually was enough for me to pay our bills and keep my family afloat for several months while I took off into the "wild blue yonder!"

## Heart Bigger Than Head!

I'd grab my guitar and follow the Star that I'd see! Sharing God's love in those out-of-the-way places where there was no financial support: jails, prisons, streets, the typical places where outcasts, addicts, alcoholics, and the downtrodden lived, etc.—that was and remains my calling!

I neglected my "one horse business" by spending way too much time working with other volunteers fixin' up that old house for Dan and Brenda Kay to move in and begin the ministry. I was totally, completely busted, that is: broke!

Dan and Brenda Kay grew tired of waiting and decided to leave town. That was a week before the house was livable. Again, God tricked me!

Even though we had Patti's teacher salary, our standard of living over the years required that I have an income as well. Since our wedding in 1969, I had always been the major breadwinner, so now, she and I were facing possible bankruptcy and foreclosure on our own home, desperately needing for me to get back to business in order to save our family from the looming hardship and heartbreak of going under.

Monday morning, home office, at my desk, my undivided attention focused on recruiting. Brad called and disrupted everything.

Brad was a 19-year-old heroin addict who had contracted syphilis. His troubled life had been a trail of broken relationships. He had burned every bridge and was sleeping in the woods. Winter was approaching.

The decision haunted me. Let go of Brad or let go of McLeod Medical and surely lose everything.

No one in their right mind would do what I did! The dreadful *"Heart Bigger Than Head"* thing blindsided me once again!

We had an available, livable house, so I went to find Brad and bring him in. He and I had two things in common. We were both sinners needing a Savior, and we were both broke!

Running on empty, I had little time to even think about or be tempted to fundraise, but bills had to be paid. I kept postponing our financial collapse using whatever available credit I could find.

During the first two years of OFA, I maxed out several credit cards, took out high-interest loans, even used the equity in our home to get another mortgage. All that was before I learned to trust God rather than credit!

On occasion, there would be a completely unsolicited donation, a love gift from a dear soul who was not even aware of the need and who had faith in what we were doing, even when I didn't!

Those unexpected love gifts not only helped keep the lights on and food on the table but also helped provide much-needed encouragement for a man who felt like such a failure and who had foolishly gotten himself and his family in a dreadful pickle! That humiliated, frightened man was obviously, yours truly.

I'd get Brad up in the morning and put him to bed at night. I'd take him to the health department. We'd visit other potential rehabs with a lot more resources to help him. None of them worked out. I was stuck with him! He and I would work on building a porch on the old house and anything else just to keep him active and productive.

All during the day, I would be sharing God's Word with Brad as he was able to receive. Some days I wouldn't even mention it. Like many in the Bible Belt, he'd heard so much self-righteous preaching, he would "shut down" and not even listen, so I didn't go there.

I was so idealistic and void of wisdom that I turned no one away. What Jesus had done for me, He would do for anyone! I didn't care if the one in need was a serial killer, terrorist, Ku Klux Klan, Black Panther or Mexican-drug-cartel kingpin! Everyone was welcome!

## Heart Bigger Than Head!

If you're going to be stupid, you'd better be tough! And *"Heart Bigger Than Head"* sure looks stupid most of the time! And I was about to find out how un-tough I was!

My every waking hour I had to be at OFA! Trapped in between the "ideal versus the real," trying to sort it all out as I kept welcoming tormented souls to move in.

In a short period of time, some of our residents would run away. With others, I would have no choice but to show them to the door or have them arrested, hoping I would never see them again, but suspicious that I probably would and on occasion, sure enough! Like a homing pigeon, here they'd come again. And yes, more times than not, I would welcome them in again! I suspect not having to pay for room and board brought some of them back. *Heart bigger than head*, dumb me—or so it appeared!

First, I welcomed Brad; then homeless-crack-addict Tom; then, Johnny, just out of jail; then Willy, who'd conned his way out of a mental institution; then, Bryan, who had been living under a bridge and eating from dumpsters; and on and on. That little house soon became very overcrowded. Stress kept mounting until critical mass! All hell broke loose!

Brad ran away without saying thank you or goodbye. Someone said he joined the circus and hit the road. Who could blame him? Gypsies, tramps and thieves, lions, tigers, and poisonous albino snakes had to have been better and less-stressful company than the OFA nuthouse!

Loud noises throughout the night, fistfights, thefts, threats, drugs smuggled in, vandalism, phone ringing off the hook night and day, outraged neighbors! I was broke, and I was to blame! That was 1996.

My own self-will was crushed! I was a totally nervous, mentally and theologically broken-down man! On my knees, crying out to God, I begged for help when, softly and tenderly, this half of a verse began to quietly surface from the depths of my subconscious mind:

**1 Corinthians 13:8 b "LOVE NEVER FAILS!"**

What?? So simple a child can see it, but at the same time, so simple, a Bible scholar walks right past it! I realized for the first time that we have a total misconception of that word LOVE!

Considering all the broken lives, dysfunction, disastrous and toxic relationships, we obviously need a total redefinition of that word, "LOVE," and "we" includes "me!"

*"Heavenly Father, redefine love for me! Teach me what real love really means, and I will come to the Light and with Your help walk it out!"* was my prayer in that moment and, after all these years continues to be.

**1 Thessalonians 4:9 . . .**
**for you yourselves are taught by God to love one another;**

## Rest Assured

*I find myself struggling to find my way.*
*I find myself fighting to make it thru another day.*
*Is anybody there?*
*Does anybody care for me?*
*Then I stop, consider Jesus.*
*I stop, and He quietly says to me,*

*"Rest Assured, I love you.*
*Rest Assured, I'll see you through.*

## Heart Bigger Than Head!

I know the sea is raging.
The roaring lion is raging, too
But you can Rest Assured.

My love is greater than life or death.
The greatest treasure is discovered
When there's nothing left but Me."

## Pocket Tees and Lee's

Coat and tie never did fit.
I was out of place and didn't like it a bit.
The reverend tag and the pulpit never was me.
Decided with the time that I got left
Gonna quit pretending, just be myself.
Sometimes it scares my wife to death,
But I suspect she still loves me
Even in my Pocket Tees and Lee's.

Pocket Tees and Lee's
Faded and frayed at the knees,
Not by the factory but by hangin' on me.
Pocket Tees and Lee's
Goin' with the wind,
Life is a breeze.
I only want to know that my Father is pleased.
I'm in my Pocket Tees and Lee's.

*God bless the steeple people,*
*I love them all*
*But a man's got to get up and go*
*To where he's called,*
*Prisons, streets, and jails,*
*A yard from the gates of hell,*
*I grab my guitar and I follow the star that I see.*
*Jesus loves me*
*Even in my Pocket Tees and Lee's.*

*When it's time to put this guitar down,*
*Lay these remains in the ground.*
*Sure be blessed with this one request,*
*"Would you bury me*
*In my Pocket Tees and Lee's!*

# CHAPTER 12

## *What is Our Father's Arms?*

The total death of self-sufficiency, becoming physically, emotionally exhausted, broken, down-for-the-count, headed for what looked like a personal disaster not for just me, but Patti and our family as well, brought me to a place where I began to realize how futile and nonproductive it is to blame anyone, including myself!

It looked like I had totally blown it, but God knew my heart! I meant well. I was just awkward, immature, impulsive, ignorant, looking stupid, and fearful, but I was trying the best I knew how!

I was in what seemed to be the self-inflicted consequences of foolish, *heart-bigger-than-head* choices, a completely unplanned dilemma; being responsible for a group of mentally ill, dysfunctional, lost souls in a residential ministry with no money, no plan, no support, no staff, and no idea what to do next! The experienced experts left town; and lost, homeless souls started showing up! And I was suffering from the *Heart-bigger-than-head* disorder!

The prayer of desperation began to open my eyes, and I begin to realize that I was enrolled in the school of unfailing Love! I started dying to trying and learning to be a branch, not the Vine! **John 15:5, Galatians 2:20.**

I started learning to "Let," not "Make." By the way, that's the difference between Isaac and Ishmael.

The School of Christ! He's the Almighty One Who is the Living Word, unfailing Love personified, not only by His Spirit teaching us how to overcome but empowering us to do it!

That is our sole purpose for being here on Planet Earth, every human being, living in these bodies on this planet in time and space, from the cradle to the grave! We're in the school of Christ but don't realize it until we get to the end of the rope, the gift of desperation, the total collapse and death of self-will!

Every trial, every crisis, every apparent problem is nothing more than an opportunity for our Lord Jesus Christ to demonstrate His faithfulness and His unfailing Love that never, ever fails! Indeed, every Calvary has a Resurrection! Heaven is birthed in the Earth through hell! Hell is for purging and purification! Selfish Willie (Self-Will) is based on a lie and not allowed into God's Kingdom and must, therefore, die! The intensity of hell is proportionate to the degree of self-will.

Since that defining moment, broken on my knees, our Lord has had my undivided attention. I consciously look for Him in every day's circumstance, every individual whose path we may cross, every event—private, personal, and global. Every detail of life is so full of object lessons in His classroom as He continually teaches us to live the self-denying freedom of unfailing Love!

Our Lord also brings to mind past experiences, those times when He did not have our attention, in order that we might see our past in a different light, continuing the educational process, helping us to see.

## What is Our Father's Arms?

The OFA Ministry began with no model or blueprint. We literally, flew by the seat of our pants with His Spirit letting us know as we go! The lesson plans are at the Teacher's discretion, not the student's!

In every decision we make, our only ambition to please Him! **2 Corinthians 5:9** Obedience to the living Word is not necessarily the same as obedience to man's interpretation of the Bible, the written word.

Oftentimes, the Living Word will lead us to make a decision that contradicts traditions and men's interpretation of the Bible. As soon as we are willing to obey the Living Word, He then illuminates the written word, and we see that there is no contradiction at all—instead a perfect complement.

It's also vital to realize that I cannot obey Him until I hear Him, and I cannot hear Him if I'm not listening!

Each of us must take time each day alone with Him, letting our souls get quiet, becoming increasingly more intimate with Him through His written Word and allowing Him to convict, cleanse, and guide! The peaceful, joy-filled sacred prayer of simply listening is powerful, incomparable, and invaluable!

Our Lord resists the proud but gives Grace to the humble, **1 Peter 5:6,7.** I will humble myself before Him privately, or it will be necessary for Him to humiliate me publicly! Either way, humility is Love's way of preparing our hearts that He may impart to us His Grace, which is His unmerited favor—but not only that! Grace is the inner strength necessary to overcome.

OFA has been called homes of healing and hope for individuals and families in crisis. We've also been called a residential rehab and even a halfway house, homeless shelter, safe house, and prison re-entry home plan. Each of those labels to some extent are true but only partially.

I think it would be more accurate to say that OFA is a place of R&D—Research and Development of unfailing love.

In industry, R&D is defined as *"work directed toward the innovation, introduction, and improvement of products and processes."*

Love is a process and mankind's application of unfailing love could certainly use some improvement. Wouldn't you agree?

The OFA R&D Laboratory is not limited to Jacksonville, Alabama, or any specific location but throughout the world, as well. Our Father's Arms are wrapped around and through this planet, though not yet recognized in some places.

The work and application of OFA over the years has turned out to be in a variety of areas, including not only homes, but also prison and jail ministry, free urgent care clinic, dental aid, concerts, broadcasting, publication, music hall, production and recording studio, scholarships, help for widows, orphans, etc.

New areas are always being considered and implemented. Overcoming and helping our neighbors in need without fanfare can really cause heartbreak, but it can also bring a lot of joy!

Several years back, this became the policy statement of the OFA homes:

> *Believing that all human dysfunction is the result of personal rejection and that true healing is possible only through acceptance, personal validation, and affirmation (God's love), we are surrendering and listening for the continual guidance of our Lord Jesus Christ in providing a family and home environment which is a place of healing, an atmosphere of acceptance (God's love), which always results in peace and tranquility.*

## What is Our Father's Arms?

*We believe that correction should never be communicated in a way that would demean another. Anger, accusation, harsh criticism, and profanity are not in keeping with our purpose.*

*Individual dignity is to be honored at all times. Each one of us is a "work in progress" learning from our mistakes. We must accept and respect each other, imperfections, mistakes and all.*

*While we do not condone rebellion and selfish inconsideration, we do attempt to exercise tolerance to a reasonable degree as God directs and enables.*

*The corporate organizational chart is turned upside down. All authority is based on being a servant. There is no assigned status of one person over another. As much as possible, we stay away from titles.*

*Conflict resolution begins with the mutual agreement that all of us are wrong. Jesus is right; therefore, there's no "taking sides" or arguing over "who's right and who's wrong."*

*God's Word, the Holy Bible, interpreted in the framework and context of His unconditional, suffering, and forgiving love, is our final authority.*

*We believe He has given us these foundational verses that we're to keep in mind at all times:*

**1 Corinthians 13:8**
"... love never fails."

**John 15:12**
"This is My command, that you love one another as I have loved you."

***1 Peter 3:9***

"Do not repay evil with evil or insult with insult, but with blessing, because to this you were called so that you may inherit a blessing."

## Let Me Love You

*Working for Me is not the same as working with Me.*
*I want you to see, I long to live My life thru you.*
*I'm not really interested in your ministry.*
*I'm not really interested in how busy you can be.*
*My interest is in you.*

*So, Let Me Love You, Let Me Love You*
*Let Me lift you high above your fears.*
*Let Me Love You, Let Me Love You*
*Let Me give you eyes to see*
*And ears to hear Me speak.*
*Let Me Love You*

*Child, you've been striving for so long,*
*Fighting to find a way to feel like you belong.*
*But can't you see I love you just like you are*
*And I've already freely given you*
*The very thing you've been grasping for.*

# CHAPTER 13
## Life is a Matter of Perspective

*Pat*

Only a few weeks after our first resident, Brad, came to live with us at OFA, two young boys were playing in the woods next to Pelham Plaza Shopping Center. They came upon what appeared to be a corpse: a smelly body that was gaunt, filthy, covered with flies, and lying motionless on the ground. Next to the body were several Lysol aerosol cans punctured with an ice pick that was lying beside them.

The boys ran out of the woods and found a police officer.

"A man's been killed! His body's over there in those woods!"

"Now calm down. Show me where he is."

Spooked, and as cautious as if they were tracking through a haunted forest at Halloween, the boys led the officer to what they thought was the crime scene.

"Over there. There he is," one of them whispered, voice trembling.

The boys watched from a distance as the police officer, ignoring the stench, knelt down and gently pressed two fingers against the neck of the lifeless body. A pulse! Immediately he radioed for an ambulance.

The man on the ground's name was Pat. He was rushed to Regional Medical Center and regained consciousness a day later. In two weeks, his vital signs were stable enough for him to be discharged from the hospital.

Pat's lifeless body

He had nowhere to go except back to another grocery store to shoplift more cans of Lysol, an ice pick, and then back to the woods with his drug of choice. Lysol is 79% grain alcohol. He was turned on to it by another alcoholic in a rehab, years earlier. It was now all he lived for.

A nurse in the psychiatric unit had heard about OFA. She phoned and asked if I would let Pat come live with us. Dang! Another *"Heart Bigger Than Head"* ambush!

"Sure, when can I come get him?"

"He'll be discharged tomorrow morning at 10:30."

"Sure. I'll see you then."

Now, Brad would have a housemate. Here comes Pat!

## Life is a Matter of Perspective

 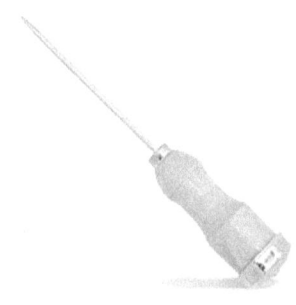

**Pat's drug of choice**

I was there on time. Regional Medical Center, fifth floor, psych ward 10:30 a.m. There Pat stood, head down, ashamed, embarrassed, and humiliated.

"Hi, Pat. I'm Bob," offering him the right hand of friendship.

He paused, no eye contact. Reluctantly, he held out his hand. It was like holding a piece of soggy bread. He quickly pulled his hand away when I let go, never looking up.

The nurse handed me a slip of paper.

"This is Pat's prescription. It's very important that he take these," she said.

I sensed that she had as much sympathy for me as for Pat. I later discovered why, and justifiably so. Pat suffered from severe mental illness. It didn't take long for us to realize that.

Pat and I were on our way to his new home at OFA, but first we needed to take care of getting his meds and a bite for lunch.

What do you do when the money's all gone and there's a need? I had not yet learned to trust God instead of Master Card. We flew in and out of the drug store on plastic wings, $36.78 to be exact! Then, since it was lunchtime, why not? Chinese Buffet, $5 a plate, iced tea, a dollar more.

On the way to the old house, Pat mumbled, "That ain't right."

"What's not right, Pat?"

"It ain't right for you to buy my medicine and lunch. A man's not worth livin' if he doesn't earn his keep and pay his own way!"

Pat was a tormented workaholic and insisted that everyone else be. I soon realized that he had a very high IQ. He told me that he'd finished top of his class and had been voted *"Most Likely to Succeed"* in his senior year of high school.

In between chores, he was constantly reading the newspaper and paperback novels, the kind that the drugstores sell.

One day while living at OFA, Pat disappeared. We found him several hours later under the house in the crawl space. He was lying there unconscious, in his own excrement. Next to him were the Lysol cans with that little hole in the side. He had smuggled them in during a trip to the grocery store. From that time on, someone else went with me to buy the groceries!

Pat saw life as his enemy. He was intolerable, opinionated, judgmental, critical, whiny, and never one to admit failure. He was ungrateful and quick to bite even the hand that was feeding him.

We kept forgiving and enduring Pat, trusting that somehow, someway, someday, he would stop fighting, let God love him, and find his way. Pat was with us for about a year. He got offended that I asked him to cut the grass instead of allowing him to sleep late.

I last saw him with nothing but the clothes on his back, walking south on Highway 21, even after we offered to buy him a bus ticket to anywhere. Again, Pat saw life as his enemy.

## Life is a Matter of Perspective

### Dannie

There were others we took in after Pat, and I thought we were at capacity—that is, until Dannie Called.

"Bob, this is Dannie! Do you remember me?"

I tried to remember. Dannie? Oh, yeah. Several years ago, he was the one sitting quietly in the corner of that smoke-filled, filthy room while the other drunks wouldn't stop preaching, all at the same time getting louder and louder! Miserable place! I think I got in one song that night!

Back in those days, our alcoholic friend, Ken, had invited me to share in a Bible study each Tuesday night in different homes. It would probably be more appropriate to say, "houses" rather than "homes." And they were dope houses at that!

Ken told me he was going to take out an ad in the local paper:

> "Come hear Bob, the Country Gospel Music songwriter pick his guitar and share in a Bible study every Tuesday at 6. High-crime neighborhood. Smoke-filled crack house on the corner. Drunks, crack heads, meth cookers, pushers, jail and prison escapees, everyone welcome. You may not need it, but, just in case, bring your own gun and knife!"

Each week, with guitar in hand, I found myself in the company of sick, wounded, practicing addicts, some of them amused by the novelty of a sober, singing preacher who didn't have enough sense to find a respectable place to preach.

Seldom was I able to get in a word, but, on rare occasions, I was able to share a song and Scripture without interruption. I determined from the beginning that I would never leave without praying for each of them, and that, I was faithful to do.

When Dannie's call came years later, I realized for the first time that those unpleasant, seemingly out-of-control meetings were not in vain after all. Once again, I realized that the "Glory of God is behind a door called 'dread.'" We just may not see it right away.

Looking back, it's a wonder we weren't invaded and "busted" by the County Sheriff's Drug Task Force! I'm so grateful that I never had to call Patti with that one phone call they let you have after you've been arrested! I'm also grateful Ken never got around to taking out that ad in the newspaper!

Dannie's call reminded me, that even though he was an alcoholic, he seemed out of place in that dope house. The only time I remember him saying anything was when he defended me as I was being mocked and ridiculed.

"Sure, I remember you, Dannie. What going on?"

"I really messed up. Started drinking again. Jessica left with the kids. I'm homeless, nowhere to go. Please help!"

"Dannie, we're full. Don't have any more room. Why don't you go to the emergency room? Surely, they'll help you detox and maybe refer you to someone who can help!"

"Bob, I don't have any money! Please help! Please!"

"I'm sorry, Dannie. We can only accommodate so many! Now I told you we were full!" Silence. Then—"Alright, damn it! *Heart Bigger Than Head* again! We'll somehow make room. where are you? Stay put. I'm on my way."

He waited at the phone booth from where he made the call. A few minutes later, I pulled up, he got in, and I rolled down the window to help ease the stench of cigarettes, booze. and body odor. I hurriedly drove him to the OFA home.

## Life is a Matter of Perspective

After introducing him to Pat and the others, we tacked up bed sheets over the entrances to the small dining area (I had gotten good at (that), and it became Dannie's bedroom. Then, I was off to find him a bed, dresser, clothes, towel, and toiletries.

We tried to keep Dannie hydrated and fed, and let him sleep for a few days. A week or so later, I was able to get him a minimum-wage job with a friend who did construction work.

While visiting the OFA home one evening, I noticed pictures of Dannie's children on his dresser: a little boy, Mikey, age five, and a girl, Misty, age seven.

"I miss them so much," Dannie said through the tears.

"They deserve more than a drunk for a dad. I've let them down and will probably never see them again."

"Dannie, can their mother, Jessica, be reached by phone?" I asked.

He pulled out his wallet, opened it, removed a wrinkled, dirty, stained corner of a sheet of notebook paper, and handed it to me. It had a smeared, faded number scribbled on it with a dull, unsharpened lead pencil.

"Here's her brother's number. Maybe they're with him."

I called Jessica that evening to let her know that Dannie had been with us for a month or so and that he was sober and working.

"The children have been asking about him," she said.

"I have no problem with him seeing them, but I refuse to let them be around a drunk."

"Jessica, why don't I bring Dannie to Germania Springs Park tomorrow afternoon; y'all can visit, and I'll also get to meet you. I've heard a lot of good things about you."

Germania Springs is a city-owned, small park with a playground for children, just north of town.

In **Matthew 18:3**, we read where Jesus said that, for any of us to enter the Kingdom of Heaven, we must become like children. As soon as Mikey and Misty saw their daddy, they started running as fast as they could toward him, arms raised and excited! No shame, no embarrassment, no problem! They loved their Daddy, and did he ever love them!

Jessica and I sat on the concrete picnic table and got acquainted as we watched Dannie, Mikey, and Misty slide, and see-saw, playing and laughing!

That was a new beginning. Jessica and the kids became regulars at the OFA home and meetings. Dannie and Jessica were officially married January 1, 1998. I had the honor of performing the ceremony, the first OFA family wedding. Mikey was his daddy's best man, and Misty was her mom's matron of honor!

One day I noticed Dannie's complexion was turning yellow. A local doctor agreed to run tests for no charge. Dannie called me after getting the test results.

"Bob, it's cancer of the pancreas. Doctor Jones said that I've only got ninety days at the most to live." He made it to only 60 days.

Three days before his death, Dannie, Jessica, and the kids came to our regular 2:30 Sunday-afternoon meeting. Dannie needed help walking. Leaning on Jessica, they made their way to the sofa.

It was obvious to everyone that he was at death's door. His eyes were sunk back in his head. He was as pale as a sheet. His body was already a skeleton and his face, a skull.

During the meeting, his head fell backward, eyes rolled back, and mouth opened. I honestly thought he had died. I put my guitar down and made my way behind the sofa where they were sitting. As I put my arms around Dannie and Jessica, he twitched and woke up. A bit embarrassed, he apologized.

## Life is a Matter of Perspective

"Oh, I'm so sorry. I just got warm and comfortable and dozed off. I'm so sorry."

"No, Dannie, don't mind. It's okay. Do you have anything to share with us this afternoon?"

"Me?" he asked, surprised that I had asked him.

"Sure. Go ahead."

He had everyone's undivided attention.

He paused, cleared his throat, and, with his frail, weak voice, said, "I'm amazed at how much God loves me. I'm here surrounded by the love of my family and friends. I know He can heal me physically, but it's okay with me if he doesn't. I'm really looking forward to the future! And I love all of ya'll!"

He then said it again, "I'm amazed at how much God loves me!"

Two days later, with his family by his side, Dannie breathed his last.

We saw our brother, friend, and OFA family resident, Dannie, make friends with life, find his way, so to speak, and die with so much grace and peace.

The other OFA resident, Pat, kept refusing to let us befriend him and be a part of our family. We don't know what happened to him.

What's the difference between these two men? What can we learn from Dannie and Pat?

That question was answered for me the evening before Dannie's funeral. Family and friends had gathered for the traditional viewing of the body and personal condolences of friends.

Brenda, Dannie's twin sister, was standing in a corner crying uncontrollably. As I approached her, she looked up and reached out toward me, sobbing. As I held her, I began to cry also. And then, as if someone had turned on a light, I saw it!

"Brenda, you and Dannie are twins! Which one of you was born first?"

"Dannie was born thirty minutes before I was."

"Perfect! That's it! Of course, there's no way you could remember it, Brenda, but for thirty minutes, then, you felt the same loneliness, emptiness, grief, sorrow, and fear that you feel now.

"Your constant companion of nine months left you there alone. It appeared that he died! When in reality he didn't die at all. He was born into a higher, more glorious life! That is exactly what has happened now. Dannie did not die! He was born! And we will be born into the higher life one day also."

When I got home, I began to search for and study all the Scripture I could find referring to "birth pains!"

Birth pangs, in terms of Bible prophecy are the wars, rumors of wars, nation rising against nation, natural disasters, etc. These are likened to the contractions experienced by a woman about to give birth, with those episodes increasing in frequency and intensity.

Jesus foretells of these birth pangs in His Olivet Discourse on end-time things to come. See **Matthew 24.**

**Romans 8:23,** *"We know that the whole creation has been groaning as in the pains of childbirth right up to the present time."*

In order to make friends with life, one must shift from the *"lower placenta perspective"* to the *"higher purpose perspective."* **Colossians 3:2**.

Drawing conclusions about life based on our limited, finite senses and perception is to draw the wrong conclusions!

From that *"lower placenta perspective,"* it appears that there's no hope. If there is a God, he's a cruel monster, a bully, and a serial killer! Would a loving father allow his children to suffer and die like we do, oftentimes without notice? A truly loving father would not allow that!

There's a continuous cry—a scream, even—echoing from this planet continuously: a mother burying a child, a tornado wrecking a community

## Life is a Matter of Perspective

and slinging human remains through the air as if they are nothing more than tree bark! Don't tell me we're loved! Life is the epitome of cruelty! Or, so it appears from the *"lower placenta perspective."*

Many of us in Calhoun County, Alabama, well remember Palm Sunday 1994. It was when Goshen Valley United Methodist Church was surprisingly hit by a tornado while children were singing: *"He's got the wind and the rain in His hands"*—and then the winds and the rains killed them!

It appears, to an intellectually honest, rational mind, one that recognizes and refuses to submit to religious superstition, that life is a merciless, vengeful, consuming beast! How, then, does one befriend a beast that you know will torture and kill you and your loved ones, often with no warning?

Remember, things are not the way they appear to be! We draw the wrong conclusion when we look at life through our very limited, finite sense of reason—again, a *lower placenta perspective*!

Pat's mind was on the end of the Earth (**Proverbs 17:24**) His perspective was *Placenta!* He had no hope! A cornered, rejected, abused, terrified creature who thought his only way of escape was a can of Lysol and an ice pick!

Dannie's view of life changed to the *"Higher Purpose Perspective."* He found hope as he allowed our Lord to embrace him, imparting to him the grace to embrace even his Earthly departure.

Jessica told me later that she and the kids were by his bed, singing with him old hymns they remembered from their childhood.

"On a hill far away stood an Old Rugged Cross, the emblem of suffering and shame. *'Twas on that old cross, the dearest and best for a world of lost sinners was slain . . ."* and then, at peace, Dannie breathed his last.

The kids are grown now. Jessica passed a few years later. She's with Dannie now.

How does one make friends with life? Simply turn your attention to the Cross and the innocent God-man suffering and dying there. All of our agony, pain, and death itself are the result of mankind's rebellion against Him.

He took all the judgment that you and I deserve upon Himself, in order that we might know Him, have Him live in our hearts, be to each of us the Shepherd David spoke of in **Psalm 23**. We then begin to see life from the *higher-purpose perspective.*

"Goodness and mercy will follow me all the days of my life, and I will dwell in His house forever."

How do I know? I don't know how I know. I just know I know. And I know, like our dear friend Dannie, that life, eternal life, is my friend. Revelation, not reason.

Thank you, Dannie. See you on the other side!

We love you, Pat, wherever you might be! Hope to see you, too!

These song lyrics came to me the night before Dannie's funeral. I used the names "Billy" and "Bubba" instead of "Dannie" and "Brenda."

## Perspective

*Billy and Bubba,*
*Twins in their mother's womb.*
*Billy and Bubba,*
*Nine months sharin' the same playroom.*
*Snug and warm, safe from harm,*
*You might say everything was cool,*
*Laughin' and a-splashin'*
*In their own indoor swimming pool!*

## Life is a Matter of Perspective

*Then Billy heard a groan*
*Bubba felt a pain.*
*Billy said, "Bubba, don't leave me alone.*
*Life without you just won't be the same!"*
*Bubba said, "Billy, I'm about to die!"*
*Billy said, "Bubba, I'm about to cry!"*

*Life is not at all what we expected.*
*Life is just a matter of perspective.*
*No need to reason why.*
*Fear not, my child,*
*Don't you know we never die?*
*What's your perspective?*

*Billy and Bubba,*
*Same room in the nursing home.*
*Billy and Bubba,*
*Ninety years have come and gone.*
*Blankets to keep them warm.*
*No cause for alarm.*
*They were washed in the blood one day.*
*No fear of tomorrow,*
*No fear of today.*
*Then Billy heard a groan*
*Bubba felt a pain.*
*Billy said, "Bubba, we're never alone.*
*Thank God the Savior came!"*
*Bubba said, "Billy, I'm about to die!"*
*Billy said, "Bubba, I'll see you on the other side."*

## CHAPTER 14
## Where Can Someone Find Sympathy?

You can shower once every hour, coat your body with any and all kinds of deodorant, but the unusual, sour, rotten-fish smell, though subtle and almost unnoticeable at first, won't go away. After a while, if someone stays too close, the repulsive body odor becomes obvious.

It's a hereditary disorder called trimethylaminuria (TMAU), a disease that impairs the ability of an enzyme to metabolize, producing an odor that can't be treated. Medical professionals agree that the odor associated with TMAU can negatively affect social and work relationships and cause severe psychological distress.

Lanny Taylor was born with TMAU. He'd also been way overweight since he was a child. The social and emotional complications of childhood obesity are low self-esteem and depression. This can be caused by being made fun of or being bullied by other children. Add to that diabetes and being born into a poor, single-parent family with no accountability, encouragement, or discipline, and Lanny had a lot working against him.

He had one thing going for him, though. He was smarter than most and had an ingenious way of adapting and manipulating his way through life.

His family and neighborhood were poor, but that didn't mean he had to be! While in high school, he went into business for himself. He called it "Lanny's Pharmaceutical Sales." When you got money, you've got friends. When you've got friends, the bullying and being made fun of stops.

Lanny parlayed his disabilities, subtly and cunningly poking fun at himself. This tended to make him very endearing, entertaining, and even fun to be around. It also was good for business. His customers and the crowd he ran with pulled him in. He became a hard-core drug user, not only selling heroin but also shooting it up.

Lanny was nearly 500 pounds. He could not walk into a room without becoming the center of attention. Candid, sarcastic, crude, vulgar at times, trying hard to conceal his big heart, but, sooner or later, the love would come out.

He loved and cared for all living creatures, including dysfunctional renegades like himself! People who love deeply hurt deeply, and Lanny, with his put-on "devil may care attitude" was a walking, wounded soul. But people naturally loved him and were drawn to him, that is, if they didn't get grossed out and run away first!

As street smart and slick as Lanny turned out to be, he was not smart and slick enough to hide from the DEA Task Force. They were on his trail, set him up, and closed in for the arrest. Even with no resistance, four officers were barely able to handcuff him, squeeze him into the back of the patrol car, and get him to the jail.

Lanny's Pharmaceutical Sales was put out of business, and its owner/CEO drug-addict Lanny was convicted and sent to prison.

## Where Can Someone Find Sympathy

The prison personnel all the way up to the warden hated Lanny, not for any reason other than the terrible inconvenience of clothing, housing, and feeding him and the other inmates constantly, viciously complaining about the odor. All Lanny had to do to get a quick release was simply be there!

After his early prison release, Lanny was court ordered to a half-way house in Gadsden, Alabama. He applied for and received a Vocational Rehab Grant to go to college. You might say, criminals and drug addicts were eligible for a scholarship for being bad! College is where Lanny and I met.

I was employed at Gadsden State Community College, Alabama, as a Computer Programmer/Analyst from 1978 to 1987. The first several years were spent helping develop and implement the automated system for virtually every aspect of the college's operations.

After implementation was completed, my responsibilities were primarily maintenance, being there to troubleshoot and repair if something went wrong. Sort of like a fireman, on-site, on-call. This allowed me time to befriend different students who would occasionally come by my office for a visit. In comes Lanny!

He and I "hit it off" right away. He noticed the Bible on my desk and began to ask questions and voice his opinion. He was borderline sacrilegious, and, when he couldn't offend me by cursing, he would come by at least every day, in between classes.

I gave him a Bug Zapper album, and the next thing you know, I was playing my guitar and sharing at the halfway house where he lived. He and I became close friends.

Lanny started bringing other vocational-rehab students to my office during the day to meet and visit. The office became a place of prayer and Bible study. Lanny and a number of others began to awaken to the forgiveness, presence, and unfailing love of our Lord Jesus.

## Learning to Love a Porcupine

I was so blessed and grateful seeing those precious students come to the light, yet I remained a bit uneasy about tax dollars supporting a Christian ministry on campus, especially during working hours. But I couldn't turn anyone away. I would come in early or stay later if necessary, non-stop. It's that *Heart Bigger Than Head* thing!

Apparently, word about the Gadsden State Community College illegal prayer room and ministry center got all the way up to the political powers that be. The "separation of church and state" gavel hit my desk, a desk that had also become an altar.

The college president sent one of his administrative assistants down the hall to tell my boss to tell me in no uncertain terms to cease and desist, so I did!

I was getting more invitations to preach, sing, and share than I had leave to cover; so, I knew it was time to resign and move on.

My older sister was a successful medical recruiter, and she offered to teach me how to do it, so medical-recruiting industry, here I come. Another "one-horse show" rode into town.

Lanny and I lost contact for at least 10 years. He graduated from GSCC with an associate's degree and went on to Jacksonville State University and earned his BS in mathematics. But, because of his appearance and odor, no respectable institution or corporation would even consider hiring him, so all he could do is call some old friends in his hometown of Huntsville. One just happened to be a bartender at the Tip Top Club.

Tip Top needed a doorman, and Lanny's gruff personality and intimidating appearance were perfect. They paid him $20 a night and all the beer he could drink. Since he didn't drink beer, they settled with him for $30 a night.

Lanny, just being Lanny, became an infamous icon at the Tip Top Club. He would sit on a bench outside, next to the front door, where he'd ID customers and take up cover charges.

## Where Can Someone Find Sympathy

A closeup of the back of a "Lanny Wear T-shirt" featuring Tip Top doorman Lanny Taylor. (Courtesy photo)

His dry wit became as much of the bar's experience as the electrifying rock music inside. Eventually a few of his oft-uttered responses to annoying customer questions were printed on Lanny Wear T-shirts also bearing his goateed visage: *"Of course I know what time it is, but it's still $5"*; *"No, I don't know where the hell the band is from"*; *"How would I know if there's anybody inside you know?"*; *"No, you can't just go in to use the damn bathroom."*

Lanny also worked for a local bookie and would take money for bets from his Tip Top bench, and frequently kept updated on game scores.

The Tip Top Club closed, and Lanny gravitated down to Pensacola, Florida, staying with a friend in his small apartment for only a few days. It became time for him to leave, with nowhere to go.

He called me one evening, ragingly depressed, regurgitating all the hurt, rejection, and betrayal of a lifetime of hopeless struggle and rejection. Time and again, he had given it his best, but he was convinced that this capricious, fickle, hypocritical, bullshit world had no place for him!

He felt justified in taking his own life, and he was going out with a broken, hemorrhaging heart, full of contempt, bitterness, and hate! He couldn't take it anymore!

Some say suicide is cowardly, the ultimate act of selfishness. They belittle, ridicule, and judge those who go that far, even condemning them to hell, but if you've never personally experienced real depression, then there's no way you'd be able to understand. Suicide is a frantic attempt to escape the dark, personal, brutal, tormenting hell of hopelessness!

Those were not cowards whose bodies were thumping the ground after jumping out of the windows of the Towers on 9/11! They were desperate to escape the hellfire of that moment!

We had to be there for Lanny! Let him know there's still hope, even after all he'd been through.

"Why don't you come to Alabama, Lanny? We've got a place for you! With your academic credentials, work ethic, and time spent in the underworld, you would be a perfect resident director for Our Father's Arms! And man, I could sure use your help!

"We just had a resident move out. The OFA house is far from being spacious and nice, but we'll make room for you. Get on up here! Do you need gas money?"

There it was again: *Heart Bigger Than Head!*

Rather than kill himself, Lanny accepted the offer. I wired him my last $40, and he headed north. As soon as he slowly pulled in, his crippled, rattling, choking, dilapidated 1978 faded-orange Pontiac that barely got him from place to place got a name: The Banana Boat. Not sure why, but it seemed to fit, so it stuck. "Here comes Lanny in the Banana Boat."

All the seats in the Banana Boat had been removed except the worn-out, stained, caved-in driver's seat. The floor looked like an old, dark-brown, dried-out banana peel covered in filthy, flaky, rust with holes here and there.

The left front shock absorber had also caved in, always looking like he was making a downhill left turn even on level ground. It belched out smoke like burning old tires covered with damp, dead autumn leaves!

The regular steering wheel had been replaced by a little 10-inch one to make room for Lanny's midsection! He was so proud of his custom steering wheel! It's the first thing he showed me after he pulled in.

Lanny Taylor in his banana boat

It was such a joy to see him! It was like a loved one returning home from a ten-year stretch on a foreign battlefield, the blessing of being reunited with a dear old friend and brother, especially one I'd been so concerned about!

He looked like he had aged at least twenty years since I had last seen him. What hair he had left had turned thin and gray. Pre-cancerous spots on his weathered forehead, wrinkles under his eyes, and the sadness. It's was readily apparent; life had continued to beat him up.

I remember thinking, He doesn't look well. He's liable to die any moment.

After Lanny moved in, he made sure everyone else knew who was boss! As soon as a new resident would come in, like a dog peeing on a fire hydrant, Lanny would mark his territory. But unlike the dog, he would do it with words, gruff words.

He never talked down to anyone while I was around, but I sure found out about it when practically everyone who lived with him would, at one time or another, call me crying and complaining about Lanny's cussing and bully attitude.

He kept a dictionary on his desk. This is how he'd welcome a new resident:

*"If you came here looking for sympathy,"* he'd growl, *"then, you can find it in this damn dictionary somewhere between shit and syphilis!"*

Surprising to me, Lanny had another nine more years to live before he would be released from a life sentence in the terribly uncomfortable, confined, painful prison cell that was his own body!

Lanny's release and relief date turned out to be March 22, 2007, at age 59. I'm sure he feels so much better now! I love and deeply respected Lanny Taylor.

## I'd Like to Recommend a Doctor

*There's a doctor for this, There's a doctor for that.*
*There's a doctor to make you skinny.*
*There's a doctor to make you fat.*
*There's a doctor to fill your brain with equations and thangs.*
*There's a doctor to give you a pill when you go insane.*
*There's a doctor for your teeth. There's a doctor for your nose.*
*There's a doctor to kill the fungus among us on our toes!*

## Where Can Someone Find Sympathy

*There's a doctor for your tummy.*
*There's a doctor for your skin.*
*Thank God for the doctor called the OBGYN!*
*Somebody call me a doctor!*
*(not that kind, though!)*
*There's a doctor for your eyes. There's a doctor for your hair.*
*Look around you friends, there's doctors everywhere.*
*Just cause you're a doctor don't mean credibility.*
*I don't want just any rubber finger*
*Pokin' around on me!*
*Be careful when you call me a doctor!*

*The sick need a physician.*
*That's the position that we're all in.*
*The Great Physician gave His life one day*
*That He might heal us from our sin.*
*I'd Like to Recommend a Doctor!*

*I went to the Great Physician one hallelujah day.*
*Full of guilt, regret, and shame,*
*I was to blame for the loved ones I had hurt along the way!*
*He showed me the scars in His hands and His feet*
*And where the sword pierced His side!*
*He said, "I came to clean you up, boy!*
*Set you free and let you be a part of My Bride!"*
*I'd Like to Recommend a Doctor!*

*He said, "When you learn from your mistakes,*
*There're not mistakes at all!*

*It's My way of helping you see your need for Me
And helping you learn to help others when they also fall!"
I'd Like to Recommend a Doctor!*

*I've got a PhD in Insanity, a specialty in Drugs'll Kill Ya!
I've done extensive research on how to wreck your life.
I could write the book on "How Not to Treat Your Wife."
I'm a master of disaster that comes when the thrills
No longer thrill ya.
I've got a PhD in Insanity.
I can help you out of your hell if you'll listen to me.
Somebody call me a doctor!
I'll simply point you to The Doctor!
His blood is an ointment.
You don't even need an appointment.
No matter how you feel.
You don't even need Obama, Blue Cross or Blue Shield!
I'd Like to Recommend a Doctor!
His Name is Jesus!*

## CHAPTER 15

# 500-Pound Man in the Basement

Over the years of sharing in countless retreats, concerts, prisons, churches of practically every denomination, giving away thousands of albums and books, we have befriended and become connected with so many dear friends here in the US and abroad, who have become family to us.

So many precious, lifelong friends who pray for us wanted to be kept up to date on what's going on. I begin sending out a periodic Communique sharing real experiences and lessons we're learning and also prayer needs. The publication is called The BrokenStone. We never ask for money.

The BrokenStone goes out only to those who asked to be on the mailing list. Periodically, unsolicited love gifts come in. Several churches began to include OFA in their mission's budget. Our mailing list continues to grow with an expanding support base.

Every donation coming to OFA has to be prompted by the Holy Spirit, because we never make an appeal or solicit in any way.

There are so many wonderful and vital non-profits helping so many people in so many ways, and we dare not compete with them for funding.

How could we afford to house, feed, and care for Lanny and others who come this way? How are we able to operate? Only by the provision our Lord sends through His children simply responding to His leading.

After Lanny moved in, we had a total of five residents. It had been two years since OFA began in Sam's house. Twenty-five precious souls had called OFA home during that time.

Sam came to our home for a friendly visit, or so I thought. He remained standing and got right to the point: "I want you to make an orderly exit out of my house."

"What? Did you not agree that you would have no expectations? Didn't we pay you five years rent in full, up front?"

"It's driving me crazy, them living up there, and my psychiatrist says I don't need that stress in my life! I'll be the bad guy! I just want ya'll out!"

I stood up, looked him in the eye, and then to his surprise, hugged his neck.

"Thank you, Sam! You providing your house has allowed us to care for 25 wounded, hurting souls who are very precious to our Lord."

"Everything under the sun eventually dies. Maybe the life of OFA was to be only two years! When do you want us out?"

His eviction notice was given July of 1998. His date for the orderly exit was to be before October 15, 1998. We had about two months.

What about Lanny? What about Johnny, Roger, James, and Dave, the other residents?

When Patti came home, I told her, "OFA has to be out of Sam's house by October 15$^{th}$."

"What?" She paused, thinking. "What if God is shutting down Our Father's Arms?"

## 500-Pound Man in the Basement

I raised my hands and said, "Hallelujah!"

She raised her hands, smiled and said, "Yes, hallelujah!"

We didn't need a psychiatrist to tell us, but the stress was taking its toll on us as well. Not only the emotional baggage of each resident and family, but our personal finances had been going in the wrong direction for too long. Bills were paid, but our credit was running out.

It looked like I needed to make some money fast, but I kept reminding myself, *"Things are not the way that they seem. There's much more than can be seen!"*

We're told in **Hebrews 11:1** "Faith is the evidence of that which is not seen." In order for us to learn to walk by faith and not by sight, it sometimes has to look like it's not working! This was one of those sometimes!

We were meeting for Bible studies each Sunday afternoon at 2:30. The next Sunday, I let everyone know.

"Fellas, we've got until October 15th to be out of Sam's house. God may be closing OFA. I want to give you notice so we can pray together about our Lord's next step for each of us."

Johnny was court ordered to OFA from the Oxford City Jail. He came to us from the same cell Ken Brown had died in four years earlier.

If we didn't relocate, Johnny would likely be sent back to jail. He was very motivated to help us find another place. The others, especially Lanny, were anxious about their future as well.

The next Sunday, Johnny brought me a picture and real estate listing.

"My sister publishes a weekly real estate ad paper. This property is going up for sale in a week or so. It may be the place the Lord has for OFA."

It looked beautiful in the picture! Five bedrooms, three bathrooms, eight acres in scenic Nances Creek. That's right! I passed by it, no telling how many times, on my way to and from Nances Creek Baptist Church! Only four miles down the same road!

It would be like coming home! I started to get excited until I saw the selling price: $136,000. We had $40 in the bank at that time.

"Patti, let's ride out there and look at it."

"Why? We don't have the money. We can't afford it."

"Well, it doesn't cost anything to go look."

So, off we go, over the mountain and through the woods to Shelton's house for sale we go! It had been A.C. Shelton Jr.'s home place, where he and his wife, Mary, had raised their four kids. Kids got grown, and Mary passed on, so A.C. built him another place that would better accommodate his bachelor lifestyle.

We turned onto the extended driveway through a canopy of beautiful hardwood trees on each side, trees that appeared to be reaching out to embrace each other above us. And then several yards further, it opens and there sits this beautiful ranch-style house with a couple of acres of manicured lawn. Wow!

We pulled to the end of the driveway, got out, and were surrounded by the sounds of country. Birds, happy and singing their little hearts out, a neighbor's dog barking in the distance. No traffic noise from a highway. The sky was so crystal-clear blue, filled with rolls and folds of angel hair, ice cream castles in the air, feathered canyons everywhere! Such a beautiful, picturesque setting.

We felt the unmistakable presence of our Lord as soon as we turned onto the property. This was God's place, but we had only $40!

No one was there, and the front door was unlocked. It felt as if we were trespassing, but we eased our way on in. When I first saw the inside, I immediately prayed, "Father, please don't let my heart go after this house!"

# 500-Pound Man in the Basement

"Patti, this would be perfect!" I kept saying as we walked through, checking out the bedrooms, bathrooms, living room, kitchen, dining area, large sitting area in the back, a huge insulated glass window with a view into the woods that was breathtaking! Then, down the stairs into the basement that would be perfect for us to add living space and a meeting room.

Again, and again, "Patti, this would be perfect" but also again, and again, "Father, please don't let my heart go after this house!"

She would simply and quietly nod and smile, also inspired by our simply being there. That was a precious, magic moment with Our Lord, my precious wife, and me. Such peace; all was well. We had a delightful tour as we sensed that this was to be the new Our Father's Arms home.

How? We had only $40 and exhausted credit. Five residents not yet able to pay rent. No way we could afford $136,000. That thought never entered our minds that afternoon.

We stepped outside to go back to the car, and, there, in the front yard, we stopped for one last look at the beauty of the place. I was reminded of the verse at the latter part of **James 4:2** "You have not because you ask not." Hmmm, I thought, we may have not, but it won't be because we ask not! I took Patti's hand and said this simple prayer out loud,

> "Heavenly Father, we ask that you provide this property to expand Your ministry of Our Father's Arms, and we pray You will do it in a way that no man would get the glory for it. Amen."

I had just written a song entitled "Reality Road."

"Patti, this driveway just got a new name! I suspect one day it will have a sign when you turn in saying 'Reality Road.'" And sure enough. It does.

I drove Lanny out there the next day, showed him around, and told him about the prayer.

"If somebody else happens to buy it, let 'um know it comes with a 500-pound man in the basement!"

We closed on that property October 14, 1998 (Patti's birthday) and never once asked anyone for anything.

We made the orderly exit out of Sam's house, and we did it by eviction date October 15$^{th}$, one day early!

And each of our residents had a much more comfortable place to call home—and sure enough! The 500-pound man was the first to move in—into the basement!

**Reality Road**

## Reality Road

*I used to live on Memory Lane*
*In a house called, Guilt, Regret and Shame.*
*Struggling with the past, I couldn't change.*
*Pining my life away on Memory Lane.*

*So, I moved to another house on Memory Lane,*
*The house of Glory Faded*
*Just as fast as it came.*
*Longing for loved ones gone,*
*Hopeless and vain,*
*In the house of Faded Glory*
*On Memory Lane.*

*So, I moved out of there to a place not so far.*
*Street sign said,*
*Anticipation Boulevard.*
*Anxiety's house, I couldn't even get out of bed,*
*Paralyzed by fear, worry and dread.*

*So, I moved to the inner city.*
*It's a pity but it's true.*
*Fussin' and a fightin' all day and all night*
*Down on*
*Anger Avenue.*
*The turmoil and strife nearly cost me my life.*
*The same'll happen to you,*
*Living down on Anger Avenue.*

*Then I heard Someone knockin' at the door.*
*He said, "The whole neighborhood's on fire, man*
*You don't want to hang around here no more!"*
*He said, "Deny yourself and follow Me."*
*I said, "Okay, from now on, You da' Boss,*
*Where we gonna go?"*
*He said, "To my Father's House on*
*Reality Road."*

*Reality Road, that's where you want to be.*
*You can know the Truth.*
*The Truth will set you free.*
*Free from the past.*
*Free from tomorrow, too.*
*On Reality Road there's a mansion for you.*

*Reality Road, all the doors are unlocked.*
*Time's not a priority here.*
*Grandfather can get rid of that clock.*
*So, Mr. Mailman, Mr. UPS, Mr. Federal Express,*
    *Uncle IRS,*
*If you got a letter or a package for me,*

*Just send it in care of my Father's House*
*On Number One, Reality Road*
*It's the first and last house on the right,*
*The one right there under the Light.*
*We stay up and praise Him all night!*
*In the front yard you'll notice*

## 500-Pound Man in the Basement

*an old, rugged blood-stained cross*
*Standing upright!*
*We receive our sight!*
*His yoke is easy*
*And His burden is light!*

*Reality Road*
*Is where you'll find whosoever will receive*
*And thank God,*
*That includes none other than me!*

## CHAPTER 16

## The Big Bank

The caller ID said, "Meridian, Mississippi." I didn't know anyone from Meridian so, as usual, I ignored it, let it ring, and didn't answer. That is until it kept ringing and curiosity got the best of me. I went ahead and answered, expecting a telemarketer.

"Good Morning."

"Good Morning. Bob, this is Ray Meyer. I want to thank you for being obedient."

"Huh? Thank you for thanking me! Obedient for what?"

"You sent me a cassette tape of a message you shared called, "Love on God's Terms." I've listened to it six times, and each time the Lord has spoken a fresh word to me."

Raymond had been born into poverty. He worked his way out beginning with the United States Air Force. He became an engineer and served during the Vietnam war as a pilot.

## Learning to Love a Porcupine

With his wife, Faith, by his side, Ray started a small business in the borrowed back corner of a cousin's warehouse. One employee—and that was him!

Twenty-five years later, their company, Meyer Enterprises, employs hundreds worldwide. The company they built from practically nothing continues to thrive and grow.

When you walk into the front foyer, the first thing you see is a large sign declaring, "Come See What God Has Done!"

Ray and I had met a few months earlier, when we both attended a Christian men's weekend retreat in the North Georgia Mountains. He and I both were speakers there.

"Bob, how is Our Father's Arms going?"

"Thanks for asking, Ray. We've been evicted from the house we were renting and will be closing down or moving. Patti and I are okay with either."

"How can we help?"

"I don't really know. Just pray and obey."

"We will pray. I'll get back with you. Good talking with you."

"You too, Ray. Hope we can visit soon."

An hour later, another call from Meridian. This time, Ray's wife, Faith, was on the line with him.

"God told us to give our house in Alabama to Our Father's Arms. Would you go check it out, pray, and let us know?"

"Really? Sure! Thank you!"

The next day their son John met us there in a rural Alabama town, about 20 miles away. We passed through a large iron gate into 24 beautiful scenic acres, landscaped around a beautiful home with multiple bedrooms and baths.

One large room was a fully equipped, state-of-the-art exercise and weight room. Another room had a beautiful, huge rock fireplace with

# The Big Bank

indoor jacuzzi. It was very nice, clean, and spacious, yet at the same time, simple and not showy or extravagant.

"Patti, are we dreaming this?"

"Our Father's Arms is going to move into our house, and we're moving into this one!" she said jokingly. We both laughed. I think it's the same kind of laughter as ninety-year-old Sarah giving birth to Isaac! In fact, the name Isaac means "laughter." The impossible happens! Awestruck! Undeniably and unmistakably, God!

After walking over the property, we met in the living room, joined hands, and began to listen and pray. Our attention was not on the property at all, but Ray, Faith, and their family were so strong on our hearts.

This was not just another luxury estate. The family pictures on the wall made it clear. We were in their home.

A little boy spending his childhood moving from one rental shanty to another, a single mom, struggling, waiting tables in cafes and truck stops, desperately trying to provide for Ray was all I could think about.

What a suffering child living in poverty goes through by being made fun of, mocked, ridiculed, wearing the same hand-me-down clothes each day cannot be comprehended by someone who hasn't experienced it!

Growing up in a world of people who think they are better than you in most cases will curse a life with hopelessness forever. But not Ray Meyer! Here we were, seeing firsthand the beauty that God can bring out of ashes! A curse, reversed!

How did that happen? How did that spirit of poverty get broken? Ray and Faith were obviously hard, diligent workers and accountable money managers, but that wasn't all! Ray and Faith walked in the favor, backing, and provision of the Most-High God!

If you want to learn to fish, learn from the ones who are catching fish! There may be experts with doctor's degrees in fishing but have never caught a fish! A tree is known by its fruit. By looking at the lives of Ray and Faith, we can learn a lot about how to live an overcoming life and be successful in financial affairs!

We knew from the moment we set foot on that property what we were to do, but we sensed we were to take a few days, listen, and be sure of our Heavenly Father's direction. I waited a week and called them back.

"Ray, thank you so much for your and Faith's generosity. Our Heavenly Father is leading us to give the property back to you and tell you to not give it away."

Silence for a moment, and then Ray replied, "We're making arrangements to move our stuff out, so Our Father's Arms can move in. Most preachers I know would have said, "Praise Jesus" and run to the bank! I knew you would listen and obey Him."

"Ray, like Abraham, you sacrificed it and got it back! There's Isaac (Laughter) again!"

"Thank you. Goodbye for now."

I'll never forget the feeling and even the amusement of that moment! We had $40 in the bank and five souls who were about to be homeless. Bills stacking up.

OFA was given an estate worth hundreds of thousands. We kept it for one week and gave it back. It's not that we refused the gift. We received it, kept it a week, and then gave it back.

Ray and Faith may not have realized it, but they were giving us much more than a piece of physical property.

They were teaching us by example a more excellent way to live and do business. God's way! **Luke 6:38:** *"Give and it will be given unto you, good measure, pressed down, shaken together and running over!"*

## The Big Bank

But this is vital: It was behind the scenes! Private! No fanfare! No advertisement or promotion! Many benefactors, even Christians, give for publicity.

In **Matthew 6:1–4**, Jesus makes it clear! *Let your charitable deeds be done in secret!*

Whenever we give, expecting nothing in return, we are making a deposit in the Big Bank. Most of the time, it's done in secret. God's Big Bank does not and cannot fail! A gift with a hidden agenda "hook" in it profits the giver nothing that will last.

Doors open and money flows according to His infinite wisdom when we are obedient! *The key is to give everything away, including our earthly life to the One we really belong to!* **Luke 14:33**. Isaac must stay on the altar!

Ray and Faith are constantly offering a lifeline to people this world has given up on. They fearlessly live at risk, providing employment opportunities for people coming out of addiction, jails, prisons, streets—and, yes, like Ray, poverty. Not only that, but orphans, widows, and "the least of them" are being helped without it being advertised! Love with no hook in it!

Do they get burned, taken advantage of, mistreated for their kindness? Stolen from, lied about, unjustly sued? Yes, all the time, but they smile and keep doing it!

Ray and Faith read, believe, and put into practice **Proverbs 19:11.** *"It is the glory of man to overlook a transgression."* Ray and Faith live in the glory of God because they are always overlooking transgressions.

There is another very valuable lesson we are learning from this precious couple. It's how to say, "No."

When the word gets out that someone has financial resources and is generous, there is a constant, growing plea and even desperate demand for help.

Often, it's a dishonest, manipulative con-man or con-woman wanting money to support an addiction. They even use their children to stir pity and take advantage.

Also, God may be getting someone to the end of their rope to get their attention and make a correction, and we must not keep giving them rope, or else we will be in rebellion and interfering with God's plan for them.

There Patti and I were, middle class all of our lives, working for a living—a common, average couple. Because of my own immaturity, we had more personal bills than we should have had, mainly because I was trusting our personal credit rather than God to keep OFA going. And in the midst of all that, we got to give away a piece of property worth hundreds of thousands! Now, how cool is that!

We had made a big deposit in Heaven's Big Bank, knowing that there would be a return, in God's timing, of course!

We have been operating out of the Big Bank since 1998, when we were shown how to do it by Ray and Faith Meyer!

Our Father's Arms has no debt and continues to be fruitful and multiply beyond anything we could imagine!

Another call. I answered right away.

"Good Afternoon."

"May I speak to Bob McLeod, please."

"Yes ma'am, this is he."

"Bob, this is Alice. I work in the office of Meyer Enterprises. We will be sending a monthly check to your ministry for $1000. How should the check be made payable, and what is the address where we're to send it?"

For a moment, I was tempted to turn it down. I had been so programmed to "be a real man and do a day's work for a day's pay."

# The Big Bank

Something for nothing doesn't line up with my and my proud family's work ethic!

But then, I was reminded of Peter refusing to let Jesus wash his feet! **Matthew 13:8**. Oftentimes, pride has to die in order to receive.

I was also reminded that the gift was to help others who had no means of helping themselves! It was to be passed on, not stored up!

I've consciously experienced true humility and gratitude many times since, but that moment was the first.

As I put down the phone, our son Scotty entered the room.

"Scotty, there's a company that's going to send Our Father's Arms $1000 a month."

"Daddy, you can buy that house in Nances Creek with that!"

"No way! God does not want His ministry to go into debt!"

Early the next morning in prayer, "Father, do You?"

I then realized the difference between creative financing and foolish financing. We were able to service a note at the bank that allowed us to purchase property worth significantly more. BrokenStone Ministries went from zero net worth to $35,000 net worth with the signing of that mortgage, a mortgage that would be paid off within just a few years.

I remembered so well the prayer, with Patti, in the front yard of A.C. Shelton, Jr.'s home place,

> *"Father, we ask that You provide this place to expand Your ministry of Our Father's Arms, and we pray You will do it in a way no man can get the glory for it!"*

So, there ya go.

## Love Not Money

*He went from rags to riches.*
*He could get a dollar out of a dime.*
*Know how to manage his time*
*But it's not greed.*
*We see him living simply*
*That others might simply live.*
*He knows how to give and help his neighbor in need.*

*It's a labor of Love Not Money.*
*Love Not Money, Love Not Money,*
*It's a labor of Love.*

*God had given us a song,*
*A melody and a rhyme.*
*Makes a soul feel fine*
*And it's been for free.*
*Now has come the time,*
*We got a new frame of mind,*
*That'll be 99 cents on iTunes*
*Ifins' you please!*
*Making music for love.*

# CHAPTER 17

## *Vance*

We were just getting settled in our new home on Reality Road when Vance's brother called.

"My family is afraid that my brother, Vance, is going to kill someone and himself! He's terribly confused, erratic, angry, and unpredictable. Please! Can you help us help him?"

Vance, even as a little boy, was obsessed with football. He became a teenager and a starter on his high school team. Even though his team usually lost, the agony of defeat could not choke the ecstasy of being out under those lights on a Friday night and hearing his name called out over that big loudspeaker!

The excitement and cheers of the small crowd of devoted family and friends really made him feel special! When he was in the 9th grade, he recovered a fumble and got his name in the local paper! That was all it took. He was officially hooked from then on, craving the attention!

The excitement of playing football also helped Vance not to think about the heartbreak of being from a broken family.

Vance's dream in life was to one day run out on the field in front of a crowd of thousands as an Auburn Tiger. So, after high school graduation, he packed his bags and headed for the Plains. (*That's what fans call the Auburn campus.*)

Vance had no scholarship, but the coaches welcomed him to be a "walk on" and suffer through every grueling practice as a defensive back on the scout team. For four years, he never got to play in a real game, but he never missed a practice!

Hanging out with the gridiron gods, at times, helped him feel special, but four years of being nothing more than a "want to be" scrub increased his already-inescapable heartbreak, insecurity, and self-doubt.

Four years of blood, sweat, and tears; of being nothing more than a "try out" was all Vance could take! If he couldn't be a football star, then he would have to "prove himself" some other way: become a fighting soldier! Surely, that would make his family and friends proud of him!

He enlisted in the *Army: 82nd Airborne Division!* He was now standing proud, and he was on his way—but not to what he expected.

In 2003 he stepped off the Army Personnel Transport Plane into the desert sands of Iraq. His company's assignment was to parachute in behind Saddam Hussein's Republican Guard and clear Highway 8 going into Baghdad.

82nd Airborne parachuting outside of Baghdad

## Vance

The Iraq Freedom War has been hailed as an easy win for the USA, but that's not all of the story.

There were battles being fought where the bodies of fellow soldiers who had become dear friends and brothers were blown apart and scattered along the roadside. The stench of death and bloody body parts were being strewn everywhere!

Vance was in the middle of it, finding himself scared speechless, trapped in a hell he never could have imagined.

He physically survived that war, yet he remained one of the casualties. He had the sanity blown out of him!

Arriving home, Vance wasn't the happy-go-lucky, fun-loving, laughing, ball-playing buddy he used to be.

PTSD is what mental health professionals call: *"Post Traumatic Stress Disorder."* It could more accurately be called: LIHSD. *"Living in Hell Stress Disorder."*

Our vision is never larger than the one person in front of us who needs help at any given time.

Looking back, I'm amazed at what we've taken on and who we've taken in! When your *heart is bigger than your head*, you find yourself doing what a so-called wise, rational person would never think of doing: putting yourself and everyone else at risk.

We consistently find ourselves in *"way over our head"* but we keep reminding ourselves that *"We're not in over our Heavenly Father's head!"*

Self-will and ungodly counsel will make one cowardly and tuck his tail, run, and hide, tormented by fear. But, trust in God Almighty, Who just happens to have ALL power and authority in HEAVEN and EARTH, changes one's perspective!

We become as fearless as the shepherd boy David, who faced and took down Goliath! Bring it on!! To the Glory of God! Bring it on!!! We're not in this thing alone!

Vance moved in with us July 2006. The first couple of days were pleasant, and we got off to a great start. He became our son, our friend, and our brother.

His sincere love for our Lord, his willingness to forgive others and himself, and his desire to work hard and contribute caused us all not only to love Vance but also to respect him. He was a precious soul.

It could not have been better. Everyone was happy and excited about the future—that is, until Vance received a check from the VA. He suddenly disappeared!

His mom was hysterical and afraid that he was dead and would never be heard from again. Imagination had us all in dreadful suspense until she received a call from the Tuscaloosa VA Hospital.

Someone had stumbled across Vance's seemingly lifeless body in a ditch off the side of a back road. They immediately called 911. After the police and EMTs arrived, they found an 82nd Airborne card in his wallet and rushed him to VA Hospital ER. A week later, his vital signs were strong enough for him to return to OFA.

It would never be the same. His restlessness, anger, insomnia, bad attitude, and confusion made him hard to live with, but our Lord's grace and love for him allowed us to endure day by day, but not for long. His next government check came. Suddenly, Vance was gone again!

A month later, we saw this on the front page of a local newspaper:

> *An Auburn man was found dead, another man was found unconscious, and a methamphetamine lab was discovered Thursday morning when the County Sheriff's Department responded to a*

# Vance

*mobile home in the Walls Bend community to look for a missing 17-year-old girl from the Athens area.*

*While searching the wooded area behind the mobile home, deputies found the body of 33-year-old Vance Davis of Auburn, the officer said. Davis's body was taken to Huntsville for an autopsy by the Alabama Department of Forensic Sciences, but it appears he died from an overdose of GHB or GBL, Savage said. The investigation is continuing."*

What Vance's family had feared, happened. No matter how much we loved him, no matter how determined we were, or the sacrifices made, no matter how much we prayed, we could not save Vance!

"What a shame! Where did I go wrong? What could we have done differently? Who's to blame? If only we had kept the VA money from him. If only we'd had him locked down. If only . . .."

We are learning that these wicked, hopeless, tormenting thoughts and discussions are illegitimate and rooted in doubt and fear, not reality!

We must stay focused on our Lord. Our mission is not to keep someone from dying! Our mission is not to alleviate suffering. Our mission is not rehabilitation! Our mission is not to serve any social cause, and it sure is not to raise money for money's sake!

Our mission is very simple: to obey our Father!

Some years ago, a reporter from the U.S. was shocked when she visited Mother Theresa in the filthy stench of a gutter in Calcutta, India, and found her lovingly holding the frail, skeletal body of a man dying of AIDS.

The reporter witnessed the sick man struggle and draw his last breath.

With tears in her eyes, the reporter asked, *"Mother, how can you keep on doing that?"*

*"My dear, when I'm holding him, I'm holding the body of Jesus,"* was her reply as she quietly moved on to take up another sick soul needing her God-given love.

Jim Elliot was one of five missionaries killed while participating in Operation Auca, an attempt to share God's love with the Huaorani people of Ecuador. He wrote this in his journal the day he was speared to death:

*"It's no fool who gives what he cannot keep to gain what he cannot lose."*

In order to serve effectively and not die prematurely of a broken heart, one must take time periodically to personally face the brevity of our physical time here on Earth. Each day, we must be willing, as much as possible, to give ourselves away to the One we really belong to.

Moses gives us the key to wisdom in his prayer **Psalm 90:12**, *"Lord, teach us to number our days that we may gain a heart of wisdom."*

**Psalm 84:5,6,7** *"Blessed is the man whose strength is in You, whose heart is set on pilgrimage.* As they pass thru the Valley of Baca (weeping) they make it a spring. The rain also covers it with pools. They go from strength to strength; each one appears before God in Zion."

One naturally gains this higher perspective when he or she turns his or her attention to behold and consider the suffering, agonizing, innocent Man dying on that blood-soaked cross 2000 years ago and what He was accomplishing there for you, me, Vance, his family, and, yes, for all of helpless humanity.

To personally, continually receive our Lord's pardon, forgiveness, and unfailing love is the only way to personally begin making friends with life!

The certain evidence is a **HOPE** that does not disappoint! **Romans 5:5**

## Having an Overcoming Perspective of Everything

# A Life of Love

*Teresa wasn't at all impressed by this world's headlines.*
*Among the diseased and the dying*
*Was where her light shined.*
*Jesus was the hand*
*Teresa was His glove.*
*She gave up the love of life*
*For a life of love.*
*Moses could have enjoyed the passing pleasures of sin*
*Until he heard the Lord*
*Calling out for him.*
*40 years in the desert*
*Learning not to push and not to shove.*
*He gave up the love of life*
*For a life of love.*

*They didn't know why Noah*
*Wasn't entertained by their fun and games.*
*A weird old fool, so uncool*
*That is, until the rain came.*
*Noah obeyed and he saved us from*
*That dreadful flood.*
*He gave up the love of life*
*For a life of love.*

*He came for His own, yet His own despised Him.*
*He bled and died on a rugged cross*

*To save us from our sin.*
*Jesus went thru hell below*
*To take us to Heaven above.*
*He gave up the love of life*
*For a life of love.*

*Whatever you possess down here you will one day give up.*
*Will you go down to the grave*
*Clinging to your stuff?*
*Or will you surrender all*
*In the arms of Love.*
*Will you give up the Love of Life*
*In exchange for a Life of Love?*

## CHAPTER 18

## Billy and Nathan

Billy's dad coached the Little League team and practiced daily with him in their backyard. It's no wonder that Billy became a star. His dad taught him the value of discipline, concentration, and hard work.

Billy's mom kept the clothes clean, pressed, and folded. Hot meals were always on the table for family breakfast and dinner. After Billy helped his mom put the dishes away and clean up the kitchen, she would help him with his homework. His mom was a teacher. No wonder he finished top of his class.

Each night, the family would say their nightly prayer, and Billy would be tucked in for the night, well fed, safe, and secure. He was given an allowance for doing the chores and taught how to tithe, save, and even invest his money.

Billy was surrounded by encouragement. He learned to believe in himself. He attended church with his family every Sunday and Wednesday. Billy met the Lord at Youth Camp one summer. He was baptized at twelve. Billy's life was blessed. Family and community, all of us were so proud of him!

**Dad pitching to son Billy**

But then, there was Nathan. He never knew his dad or granddad. His grandad was killed in a car accident years before Nathan was born. Nathan's mother, Fran, was only six years old when the tragedy occurred.

She was one of five little girls left with a mom, Irene, who had no job skills, working one minimum-wage job after another; fighting to survive; unemployment; eviction from one dilapidated rental house or trailer to another; living with roaches and rats in a cloud of "roll your own" smoke; many times electricity cut off for non-payment; a lifestyle of rejection; ridicule and humiliation; a constant struggle. There was no one there to help them.

There were no pretty dresses for Fran to wear for the junior high prom. But that was okay. She often said that she never wanted to go to the prom anyway. That was for rich kids. No need for a hairstylist. Never heard of a pedicure, and a manicure, to her, was probably medicine for a man.

## Billy and Nathan

Fran was a beautiful little girl. She matured and developed physically into a beautiful young lady. There were little boys who flocked together, hanging out like "boy dogs" at the trailer park where they lived. They were developing physically, too.

Sammy, one of the young "boy dogs" was only 15. He told Fran that he loved her. He meant it too! He kept listening to his favorite country song, "Feels So Right." And since country music tells it like it is, it's got to be right, if it feels right. It's just got to be love!

Fran believed Sammy because she wanted to. If it feels good, why not do it? Everything else life throws at you feels so wrong!

The inevitable happened. Fran, 14, gave birth to a precious baby boy. She named him Nathan because that was her daddy's name, and she still missed him.

Nathan grew up living in the same poor, pitiful nightmare as Grandma Irene, his mom, and her sisters.

Nathan had no dad to coach his Little League team, but that didn't matter, because even though he wanted to so bad, he could never play. No money for fees and uniforms. Little League is for rich kids.

The only male role models in Nathan's life were the drug addicts and dealers who kept flowing in and out on their way to prison or the cemetery, the ones who kept fighting over his good-lookin' momma who, for some reason, seemed to attract the meanest and most violent.

From the time he was a toddler, Nathan could remember weekends filled with drugs, drunks, screaming, cussin', open orgies, and knife fights.

When he was six, hiding in a corner, he watched as one loudmouth drunk sliced another's throat, killing him because he'd made a pass at Nathan's mom. Nathan was forced to hurry and help clean up the blood before the lawmen got there.

## Learning to Love a Porcupine

Fran, aged beyond her years, could no longer handle the baggage of a kid, so in one of her drug-induced, "I-don't-give-a-damn" moments, she gave Nathan away to foster care. She later hated herself for it.

Nathan was already marked. Stealing, lying, manufacturing, selling and using was in his DNA. He wasn't caught and arrested until he was thirty.

I went to see Nathan in jail, and the court ordered him to the "Our Father's Arms" family. His first day with us, he lied to me for the first time saying, *"Bob, I promise, I'll never lie to you."*

He lasted only a month. Sentenced to prison with an E.O.S. (end of sentence), 2028.

Nathan's letters from prison were encouraging. His court-appointed lawyer told me that he had never before received a letter from an inmate apologizing. We corresponded for several years, but I haven't heard from him in a while.

He once wrote me, "Bob, the Word that was shared with me at "Our Father's Arms" was not in vain. I couldn't hear it then. It took me getting locked up in prison to see the Light. I don't like it here, but this is what it took, so I'm grateful. What's left of my life belongs to the Lord. I'm serving Him in here each day. My future is in His hands."

Last I heard, Nathan was serving as the chaplain's assistant and leading a Bible study for other inmates.

We've lost track of Nathan.

What about Billy? He continues to be admired and respected. Very successful in business. He now has his own son. We're all proud of him as well. Billy remains an avid sports fan. He sits on the board of his prestigious university's alma mater board and even helps with the fundraising. I also heard that he's a deacon in his church. How blessed his life has been.

Our Father's Arms is not a home and family for the Billys. They're already taken care of, but, if you happen to come across any Nathans or perhaps an Irene who is elderly and physically falling apart, needing help and hope, a Fran whose children are still young, please tell them that there's hope and help.

Tell that young, desperate mother that she doesn't have to give her children away. Tell her that she doesn't have to hide in a pill bottle, pickle her brain with alcohol, or let men continue to use her and throw her away like last week's newspaper.

Any kids out there who want to play Little League or would like to go to the prom but haven't been able to? We're here to help and keep it behind the scenes.

**Matthew 6:4** "Let your charitable deeds be done in secret."

## No Reputation

*He drives a beat-up '66 pickup just to get around.*
*T-shirts and faded jeans when he's dressed his best.*
*Folks look down their noses at him*
*When he's passin' thru town.*
*But he ain't a bit concerned about who's impressed*
*'Cause he's got more money*
*than most banks in town.*
*He even makes loans to the Savings and Loan.*
*But he doesn't flaunt it or flash it around.*
*This dude even lives in a ten-foot-wide mobile home.*
*And his heart is humble,*
*And his life is simple,*

*even though he's come so far.*
*He avoids the people who butter him up*
*And he knows who his friends really are.*

*That's why I was born in a manger.*
*That's why I never ran around with the superstars.*
*That's why I made myself of No Reputation.*
*That's how I know who My friends really are.*

*If they'd a known I was the King of Kings,*
*Do you think they would have spit in My face?*
*If they'd a known I own it all,*
*Do you think I would have been disgraced?*
*I left a mansion in Glory, so the pure in heart could see*
*And however, you treat the least of them,*
*That's how you're treating Me.*

## CHAPTER 19

## Mother Millie

It seemed nothing more than another typical day in the projects. Little Millie was a beautiful, healthy, 18-month-old toddler. Her dark-brown eyes, smooth olive skin, and curly black hair made her adorable.

She could easily have been a child model, a cute little Native-American Shirley Temple, but that fairy tale world wasn't about to happen for little Millie!

With a cat's curiosity, awkward, pudgy, little arms held out for balance, little Millie was simply doing what toddlers do, bouncing around the room, getting into everything on a determined expedition to find anything small enough to shove in her little drooling mouth and chew on it! So cute but requiring constant care and attention.

Then suddenly, the day wasn't typical anymore! There was an unexpected deafening blast from a 12-gauge shotgun! BLAM! Little Millie started screaming!

Fortunately, her grandma was there to grab her up, hold her close, and gently pat her little back, attempting to comfort her.

Millie was too young to consciously remember, but, as the years went by, she kept having reoccurring dreams. She would be in a deep sleep when suddenly: the BLAST! She'd jump up, wide awake, terrified, heart nearly pounding through her chest, lips quivering, totally incapable of going back to sleep until the following night, when she would literally collapse from exhaustion.

**An innocent little girl in a secret nightmare**

When Millie was about eight years old, she told her grandma about the unexpected, terrifying BLAST in her sleep.

"Millie, that blast actually happened!" her grandma replied, not able to hide it any longer.

"Your mother, screaming and cursing, grabbed the shotgun, aimed it at you, and pulled the trigger! I was able to deflect the barrel just in time to save you! I'm so sorry that happened, Millie!"

Millie's mother was diagnosed with a psychotic condition known as paranoid schizophrenia, a chronic mental illness in which a person loses touch with any sense of reality. The classic features of paranoid

## Mother Millie

schizophrenia is having a preoccupation with one or more delusions and frequent auditory hallucinations (hearing voices.)

The delusional content (the beliefs) of the person suffering with paranoid schizophrenia is marked by grandiosity or persecution or both.

Anger, irritation, or argumentative behavior may be the most prominent features, along with extreme jealousy, which was certainly the case with Millie's mom.

Add the mind-altering toxins of alcohol and recreational drugs to an already unstable, mentally ill soul and the devil's torment, chaos, and destruction become jet propelled! Hell on earth is unleashed! This is the world Millie was born into! It's a miracle that she survived!

Millie's mom told her that she was conceived in the back seat of a '57 Chevrolet at a drive-in theatre. Her mom wasn't married and repeatedly told Millie that she was a mistake!

After Millie, there came five more so-called mistakes: brothers with different dads! Millie's mom was out of control!

When Millie was only five years old, her mom married and brought a strange man into their home. The children were forced to call him "Daddy."

As soon as "Daddy" found an opportunity, he took little Millie by the hand and led her into the bedroom. He closed, locked the door, and began sexually molesting her! This nightmare continued repeatedly for three years! She tried to hide from him, but he always found her.

"Shhhh! Don't forget, this is our little secret just between you and me, so don't dare tell anybody!"

One morning little Millie was bleeding, hurting, and having trouble using the bathroom. Her mother heard her crying and went in to see what was wrong. That's when the "little secret" wasn't a secret anymore.

That was Millie's eighth year. That particular monster was driven away, but others were yet to come!

Millie and her brothers were left at home one evening with a babysitter who was to stay with them all night while their mom was out partying. As soon as mom paid the babysitter and left, the babysitter took the money and left, too! She was considerate enough, however, to call the police and report the abandoned children!

The police arrived and took the children to an orphanage. From there, they were shipped out to one foster home after another, where they were repeatedly raped and even tortured!

Millie's life story continued to become even more tragic. Drugs and alcohol addiction, promiscuity, an aborted baby, being drawn to men who would beat her and one who even attempted, multiple times, to kill her.

At one point, she was hiding from DHR trying to protect her younger brothers and to keep the family together. For weeks, they lived homeless under the Courtney Campbell Causeway Bridge in Clearwater, Florida, scrounging through dumpsters for food to survive.

Millie never believed that God would allow her to have another baby after aborting her first, but He did. She gave birth to a cute, healthy little boy she named Sterling. She adored Sterling, and he became Millie's reason to live and not give up and self-destruct.

Literally running for their very lives, Millie took Sterling to a safe house in Alabama. The predator who was out to find and kill them was killed in a car accident. Relief!

In 1992, Millie began awakening to the reality that there is indeed an Almighty God Who passionately loves her, her son, and even her mentally ill mom. She began to realize the power of His cross. She received His forgiveness and His grace to forgive others, even those who had raped, misused, beaten, and tortured her and her brothers!

The director of the safe house saw potential in Millie and kept encouraging her day by day to continue her education.

Today she has a B.S. Degree in Social Services from Jacksonville State University, a Master's Degree in Counseling with certifications in Domestic Violence, Anger Management, and Parenting, and she is an active member of NAMI (National Association of Mental Illness.)

She has been free from drugs for more than 20 years and, since 2005, has been actively involved in ministry, helping get a lifeline to other wounded souls.

We know Millie as "Mother Millie" and have been privileged to serve alongside her now since 2007. She and her husband, Mike, and eight desperate ladies with no support, ladies coming out of addiction, jails, and homelessness, moved in with us at OFA that year.

Millie has become a mentor to me and so many others on how to live a Spirit-filled, overcoming life. She remains a close partner and is now focusing on counseling, teaching, and taking in dysfunctional families in crisis.

**Makalla and Mother Millie**

# Eagle With a Broken Wing

Your life is filled with pain.
You can't hide from the rain.
Did you hear them say, "You'll never fly again"?
But they can't see the eagle you were born to be,
Or the truth you came to see when you flew back then.

Eagle With A Broken Wing,
No one wants to listen
As you sing of the sights you've seen,
Or the loneliness that being broken brings,
But I know you, Eagle With A Broken Wing.

The truth is so hard for the turkeys who gobble in the yard;
Demanding you gobble, too, but you'd rather die.
You hear others who boast they can fly,
And the crowd doesn't know it's a lie,
But you dang well know
'Cause you're from the sky.

Look up.
Someone is calling you.
Your time of dying has finally come to an end.
The One you love is healing you.
Spread your wings, Eagle.
It's time to fly again.

## Mother Millie

*Oh, Eagle you had a broken wing,*
*Now they're starting to listen*
*As you sing of the sights you've seen,*
*And Eternal Life that resurrection brings.*
*I know you Eagle,*
*You had a broken wing.*

# CHAPTER 20

## Freed from Fear

Rob was known for being a gentleman, laid back, good natured, kind and forgiving toward everyone, but his wife Pat noticed that he just hadn't been himself lately. One Thanksgiving Day, it all came to a head! He could no longer take it!

Rob suddenly jumped up from the table, threw his chair back, and stomped out from the family Thanksgiving dinner, leaving Pat and his family stunned. He didn't own a gun, so he grabbed an iron collar from the bar bells as he passed thru the garage, and got into his car, foaming at the mouth like a mad dog, on his way to beat someone to death!

His daughter, Jeanie, was more than precious to him! From the day she was born, she'd brought laughter, joy, delight, and fun to life. Growing up, she was his cute little sidekick, most definitely a daddy's girl!

Rob, as a young man, had been trapped in the nightmare of alcohol and drug abuse. However, when Jeanie was a newborn baby, he repented and found a new life in Jesus Christ. That made her even more precious and endearing to him. Jeanie was a living reminder to Rob of his Lord's Grace and Mercy.

Jeanie grew into a beautiful, bright, delightful young lady. She graduated from high school, enrolled in college, and was on her way to an exciting and promising future.

One afternoon, Les, Jeanie's classmate who had become her special boyfriend, came by and asked Rob for her hand in marriage.

Since Les was the son of friends who were faithful to their church, Rob and Pat felt okay with it. Les was even a licensed minister, a young preacher.

Rob walked Jeanie down the aisle and "gave her away" to a young man he and Pat naturally assumed would love, protect, and provide for her. They were wrong!

Les, within a year, became a drug-addict criminal who began abusing Jeanie! She took her baby and moved in with Rob and Pat. There she felt safe, knowing she and her baby would be well taken care of and protected.

Les became elusive and hostile. He stole a book of Rob's checks and begin forging Rob's name to cash and buy drugs. Rob and his household were under attack. Rob was now in the combat mode! Someone was about to die!

Rob, the gentleman, had suddenly become a violent, enraged vigilante! It looked like the devil was about to win! Nothing could stop Rob! Nothing, that is, except one thing: the Jesus he had received into his heart years earlier when Jeanie was a newborn wouldn't let him go!

In the midst of the violent voices of madness and hatred screaming in Rob's deranged mind, he began to see the innocent One hanging in horrible agony on that blood-soaked cross! Hanging there for him! Hanging there for Les!

## Freed from Fear

Rob, in the midst of his emotional and mental rage, began to hear a still, small voice, whisper, **"Bless those who curse you. Do not resist evil with evil. Love your enemies. Forgive those who wrongfully use you. This is my commandment: Love like I love you."**

Rob went straight to a motel, checked in, hurried to the room, and there, alone, fell to his knees and began crying out to his Lord:

*"Please take this hatred out of my heart! I'm so helpless! I can't do it! Dear Jesus, please let me see Les with Your eyes! Dear Jesus, please help me!"*

The tears continued to flow for who knows how many hours, and then, The Light of God's unfailing love broke through!

Rob was set free! His eyes of contempt became eyes of compassion.

Now, he could pray effectively for Jeanie, her baby, and his family! He could also pray effectively for Les, the one who had chosen to become his enemy!

With no malice, Rob signed a warrant to have Les arrested for stealing and forging his checks. True Love will hold one accountable. He had Les arrested for Les's sake, not personal vengeance.

Rob went to the jail and was allowed to visit with Les privately in a cell used primarily for counsel with attorneys. Les, wearing stripes and handcuffs, and dragging ankle chains, was led by an armed guard into the cell. When he saw Rob sitting there waiting, he wanted to run but was trapped like a deer in the headlights!

Rob stood up; with tears of compassion in his eyes, he went up to Les and embraced him.

"Les, I want you to know that I had you arrested because I love you. You are forgiven. We pray and trust that this will be a turnaround for you. It's never too late."

Rob went on to share with Les about that Thanksgiving night the Lord interrupted his mission of murder.

"Pat and I love you as our son, Les, and only want the best for you." Rob prayed for him and then left.

Les was not heard from for six years. One afternoon, the phone rang. Rob answered. A thick tongue, slurred voice, full of anxiety and fear, said:

"If anyone has reason to hate me, it's you, but I ain't had nothin' to eat in three days and got nowhere to go! Nobody wants me around! Please help me! I'm so sorry for what I done! Please help me!"

"Who is this?"

"It's Les."

"Les! Where are you?"

"I'm homeless and broke. I borrowed a phone to call you. I'm somewhere on Black Gap Road."

Rob rushed to find him staggering down the road, chewing on a Morphine patch, no shirt or shoes. Rob got out and helped him into the car, drove him to Our Father's Arms, Reality Road, just a few miles away.

There, he was given some warmed-up leftover chicken and dressing from the night before. He begin stuffing himself like a starved animal. He was given some clean clothes, tooth brush, toothpaste, and shaving kit. After cleaning up, he crashed for at least two solid days. In a matter of weeks, he detoxed, reconciled with his parents, and, several weeks later, moved on with his life.

Rob, Pat, Jeanie, and family haven't heard from Les for years, but, when he comes to mind, prayers continue.

Our Lord has remained so faithful to Rob and his family, turning everything around! Jeanie and her children have a husband and Dad who is truly a man of God devoted to his family—loving protecting and providing, more than Rob and Pat could ever have wished for! Every day is Thanksgiving at Rob and Pat's house!

# Freed from Fear

## Lesson Learned:

Anger, hate, and murder are rooted in fear! Rob had, in well-meaning ignorance, possessed his precious daughter Jeanie, deceived into believing she belonged to him. That's why he felt responsible for being her savior, all the while rejecting and "stiff arming" the real Savior without even realizing it!

All fear is the fear of losing something. Anything one is afraid of losing is an idol, another god before the one and only true God.

We must seriously give heed to these seemingly impossible words of Jesus in **Luke 14:26:** *"If anyone comes to Me and does not hate his [own] father and mother [in the sense of indifference to or relative disregard for them in comparison with his attitude toward God] and [likewise] his wife and children and brothers and sisters—[yes] and even his own life also—he cannot be My disciple.*

*"So then, any of you who does not forsake (renounce, surrender claim to, give up, say good-bye to) all that he has cannot be My disciple."* AMP.

In all honesty, I can't do that! I can't surrender claim to all that I've worked so hard for in order to provide for MY family. Besides, God understands that I'm only an imperfect human!

Turning a "reason" into an "excuse" is a deadly spiritual dead end!

Jesus again: "Be ye therefore perfect as your Father in Heaven is perfect! **Matthew 5:48**

If one dares to lower the Lord's standard, spiritual growth will stop!! Then, how does one do it?

Jesus again: "Without ME you can do nothing!" **John 15:5**. God is at work in each of us, and He will accomplish His purpose. **Philippians 2:13.**

I can do ALL THINGS through Christ Who strengthens me! **Philippians 4:13.**

ALL THINGS includes letting go of the other gods before Him. To live the freedom and power of His unfailing love, we must stop resisting Him in any way! When we defensively have other gods before Him, we are like the player on the Heisman Trophy, who clings to his ball "idol" and aggressively stiff-arms anyone, including the Lord, who threatens to take it!

It's not what we do to be free. It's what we stop doing. Stop stiff-arming Jesus. If one is simply willing to "let go," then our Lord will continue to do the miracle in that person's heart, setting him or her free to live and enjoy the freedom and the power of His unfailing love!

**The stiff arm**

It's also very important to keep in mind that our Lord is not calling us to give up our loved ones. He's helping us to release illegitimate possession of them so that we can truly enjoy each other and all the other blessings of life on a non-clinging basis.

## Straining on a Gnat
### Matthew 23:24

*Whatever time brings your way,*
*Time will surely take it away.*
*Friend, family, foe, come, and they go.*
*Nothing here is here to stay.*

*Straining on a Gnat, swallowing a camel*
*Is the way we've been living our lives.*

*Making something out of nothing,*
*Nothing out of something.*
*How blind can we be?*
*Living in a panic,*
*Spit in the Atlantic,*
*We take ourselves way too seriously.*

*Living under the S.U.N. is all vanity.*
*Living under the S.O.N. will restore your sanity.*
*Life can be F.U.N.*
*We can live worry free if*
*We go ahead and let go*
*Of what we'll have to let go of one day anyway!*

# CHAPTER 21

## *Homeless Child*

A hiker stumbled across her beaten, blood-covered, naked body at the bottom of a ravine on a dirt backroad in West Georgia, just across the Alabama state line. The baby she had been carrying three months was killed when she was stabbed multiple times, thrown away, and left for dead.

That can happen when you tell a bully pimp that you're not going to let him sell your body anymore.

Hannah was rushed to the hospital and miraculously survived! After several weeks, her vital signs were stable enough for her to be released.

She was not put out on the street and left homeless. She had warrants for her arrest in Calhoun County, Alabama. Two deputy sheriffs were there to take her to jail, where she was booked and remained for a year. She was okay with that! She felt protected there!

While in jail, Hannah prayed to receive Christ and became a regular at the inmate Bible study.

The jail chaplain worked closely with Hannah and recommended she come to OFA after being released.

The time came, and Hannah moved in. We let her stay in the protected guest suite that has a private bath.

Day by day, she was very pleasant, appreciative, and helpful. She had a great attitude, an eager, hard worker with initiative, proving to be a leader.

Henry was special and incapable of taking care of himself. He was innocent, naive, and so easy to love. He was 30 years old, yet still a little boy in a 6'4", 350-pound body.

His huge potbelly pushed out the skin-tight, ragged, faded, hand-me-down, Nascar T-shirt that had become his trademark.

Henry's speech impediment made it impossible for some of us to understand him. Those who spent time with him in jail had learned his language and could interpret for those of us who had no clue what he was rattling on about. Hannah immediately picked up on Henry's language and had no trouble communicating with him.

Henry was diagnosed as having an intellectual disability and given to pyromania, an obsessive desire to set things on fire.

Several months before we met him, Henry had been made fun of, mocked, prodded, and dared by a group of neighborhood bullies to set fire to an abandoned church building out in the woods near where he and his mother, Sally, lived. They even gave him the matches.

Henry was standing there, mesmerized by the flames, when the deputies arrived and arrested him for arson. The bullies were hiding in the woods, laughing, as Henry, terrified, was handcuffed and taken to the County Jail. Several months later, Henry was released to the custody of his mother.

Henry never knew his dad, who'd died when he was a child. He grew up in an impoverished neighborhood just a few miles from OFA on Reality Road.

# Homeless Child

A builder friend and I went to visit Sally and Henry and were heartbroken when we saw their living conditions. The electricity had been cut off for non-payment. Henry's weight had been too much for the rotten floor under the bathtub that had fallen thru to the dirt crawl space.

We offered for Sally and Henry to come live with us until we could recruit some volunteers to repair their home and get the power back on. Sally refused, but with Henry's insistence, she reluctantly gave in and let him move in with us for a few days that became a few weeks. Hannah had taken to Sally and Henry like family, and they to her as well.

Hannah had become like a nurse and caretaker for Henry, which included helping him eat healthy and staying on his diabetes medication.

At noon, following lunch, they would go on a brief, daily walk on a trail through the Talladega National Forest, which adjoined our property. It also provided Hannah and Henry a way to sneak off and smoke, which is a violation of our policy.

Hurrying to get back, Hannah let Henry keep the cigarette lighter. Mistake!

## Henry's fire

That afternoon, Henry disappeared. As soon as we saw the smoke and flames in the back woods, we called 911, grabbed the rakes and shovels, and ran toward the fire. It was a dry season, and the blaze was getting out of control.

The firefighters arrived right after us, and there was Henry, standing back, again mesmerized, staring with a smile like a child watching a Disney thriller. The police were on their way to take him back to jail.

# Learning to Love a Porcupine

**Henry sets the woods on fire**

The firefighters saved the day and got the fire out, but we were all heartbroken! It was time for Hannah to go!

A friend connected us with a Christian rehab for women in Wisconsin, of all places! They had a bed for Hannah, and no up-front deposit was required.

We passed the hat, bought her a ticket, blanket, portable CD player, and gave her several CDs for the 27-hour bus ride! I suspect she was sick of Bob McLeod songs by the time she got there, but we had a few in stock that we got wholesale!

The night before we put Hannah on the bus, she and I had a special, private, few moments together.

"We love you, Hannah. Is there anything more about your life you'd like to share with me before you go?"

She told me this story:

"Bob, I grew up in a home full of hate," she said. "My mom and dad were constantly fighting and cursing each other and me, that is, until my dad got drunk, beat us both, and left. I was 6 and never saw him again.

## Homeless Child

"For some reason, my mother blamed me. She wouldn't let up. I could do nothing right. She kept telling me I was a mistake, how much I'd cost, and how she wished I'd never been born.

"I had nowhere to run until I was 16. I met a very charming, handsome man who drove a new BMW. He said he was an agent. He told me how beautiful I was and that I could have a career as a model and make lots of money. I wanted to believe him, so I did.

"It was my ticket to escape from my mother, who I hated, so I packed a few things and left with him to Atlanta. It was there he introduced me to heroin. That was his hook in me! That and me deceived into thinking that we were in love!

"He turned me over to a group of heartless men who were demons, and then, with a briefcase full of cash, he drove away in his BMW, leaving me behind. That was the last time I saw or heard from him.

"I was shaved, beaten, sodomized, raped, and sold for sex over and over again. It was 24/7 madness! It never stopped! The hell I found myself in was unbearable! They had me constantly on the move, from one state to another, trapped, with no way out!

"They forced me to take birth-control pills, but I started secretly flushing them down the toilet. When I started showing signs of being pregnant, they were furious! That's when they tried to kill me! And they did kill my baby."

Then for the first time, I saw Hannah cry.

She continued, "But God revealed His love to me and saved me for what I know is a special purpose. Thank you for letting me come here. I had nowhere else to go.

"I made a terrible mistake with Henry, and I'm so sorry, but I'm not running this time. I really do know my Heavenly Father has forgiven me and is directing me to go to the rehab in Wisconsin."

The next morning, I drove Hannah to the bus station. We hugged and said our goodbyes, and I watched as the Greyhound Bus's diesel whined and drove her away.

**Putting Hannah on the bus**

God, Who is Love, continues to teach us through everyone He sends this way.

Dear, precious Hannah, like Ken, is also a microcosm, a reflection of every one of us. Human beings *being* human beings.

Our time with Hannah inspired this song:

## Homeless Child

*She climbs aboard a Greyhound*
*Looking for a place called "Peace of Mind,"*
*Any town, more sane and sound*
*Than the one she's leaving behind.*
*She'll find another man to abuse her*
*Because she thinks it's what she deserves.*
*He'll say, "I love you"*
*Then use and accuse her.*

## Homeless Child

*She believes all the angry words.*
*She's a Homeless Child, a Homeless Child.*

*We lost a best friend outside of Saigon,*
*A mother's son on a Baghdad backstreet.*
*History keeps repeating itself*
*As the whole world continues to weep.*
*Gang war in New York City.*
*Gang war in the Middle East.*
*Innocent blood shed in our schools*
*And it's a pity,*
*The politician's a fool*
*Who thinks his party can stop the beast.*
*We are a Homeless Child,*
*A Homeless Child*

*We know a lot about livin'*
*But do we really know how to live?*
*We know a lot about gettin' even*
*But do we really know how to forgive?*
*We can't get along together.*
*We can't get along alone.*
*We can make it to the moon*
*But does anybody know the way home?*
*We are a Homeless Child, a Homeless Child.*

*Is there any hope in this world?*
*The motivational speaker smiles, says, "Yes"*
*Right before he passes the plate and dies.*

## Learning to Love a Porcupine

*We must look beyond the sunset*
*If we're to dry our weary eyes.*
*Peace of mind is in Our Father's Arms.*
*He reaches through a cross,*
*Calls you His friend.*
*The Commander-in-Chief shed*
*His own innocent blood!*
*Welcome to the Kingdom that will never end!*
*Come home, My child!*

*Softly and tenderly, Jesus is calling . . ..*
*Ye who are weary, come home.*

## CHAPTER 22

## He Put Sue Aside

George Culhane wrote me from the Calhoun County jail. His letter was articulate, to the point, and struck a chord of sincerity and compassion. We get stacks of letters from the jail, but this one was different. It gave me a natural curiosity and interest in George.

I phoned Ms. Moody, a certified counselor with a master's degree and a successful practice at that time. She had done a psychological assessment on George.

"Ms. Moody, do you recall doing a psychological evaluation on an inmate named George Culhane?"

Pulling his file wasn't necessary. How well she remembered him! She was personally indignant and adamant, she related in no uncertain terms, how he had been mistreated,

"Bob, this dear man is 66 years old, a professional who has worked hard all of his life, provided for his family, no previous criminal record.

Yes, he once had a drinking problem but successfully dealt with it, and now some members of his family are using it against him. There's a great injustice going on here, Bob. Please help him if you can."

I went to the jail to meet and visit with George.

John, the jail administrator, was standing at the door of his office as we passed by. I quickly shook John's hand as usual and greeted him,

"Good morning, John. Keep up the good work. See ya later."

John had been given an impossible task. Understaffed and underfunded, he was responsible for all the activities involved in warehousing hundreds of dangerous people. The dreadful, depressing confines of concrete hemmed in by a 10-foot chain-link fence, topped with rolls of razor blade barbed wire wasn't a vacation place!

Different men and women from different cultures, different nationalities, different neighborhoods, different gangs, different religions, different medical needs, different charges, but all in the same nightmare, pressed together like sardines, with more being arrested, booked, and added to the number every hour of every day! No wonder John seemed depressed and stressed!

"Who are you coming to see this time, Bob?"

"George Culhane."

John motioned me into his office.

"Have a seat, Bob. We need to talk."

"Sure. What is it?" I said as I sat down in the old, faded-gray Army surplus metal chair next to his desk.

"Bob, you've got a great thing going out there at Our Father's Arms. People are being helped, and lives are being changed. I'd hate to see it jeopardized. I'd strongly encourage you not to have anything to do with George Culhane!"

"Really? Why's that?"

## He Put Sue Aside

"He's a sociopath. He has no conscience. He'll be nothing but trouble, and he'll intentionally undermine everything you're trying to do. He'll stab you in the back, Bob. I don't want to see you and Our Father's Arms get hurt."

Knowing John was also a certified counselor, I certainly respected his advice.

"Since I'm already here, I might as well meet with him, if that's okay."

"Go ahead, but be careful, and don't let him pull you into his trap."

"I'll try not to, John. Thanks." Another deputy escorted me down through the noisy, concrete corridor into the spiritual darkness where the criminals are confined. We passed through three massive sliding steel doors into the cell used for private interviews.

As the door slammed shut, locking me in, I suddenly realized what it would be like to be buried alive in a concrete cemetery vault with no air and no escape! The claustrophobic panic of suffocation began closing in. I refused to let myself think about it!

Instead, I began to reflect on John's words and whispered a prayer, "Lord, please help me not to be manipulated and controlled by sympathy." I learned years earlier, the hard way, that sympathy is a deadly perversion of compassion and empathy! It's the co-dependent controler's favorite trap. If anyone can get you to feel sorry for them, they've got you under their control!

Then, suddenly the thick metal door to the cell began to slide open, and there he stood: George, himself! He was handcuffed, with his feet chained to each other, as if, without them, he could run through four metal doors, past 13 armed guards, and then jump over that 10-foot fence topped with another three feet of razor blades!

George looked so out of place. He was a distinguished-looking, elderly gentleman who should have been in a business suit rather than an orange jumpsuit with "County Jail" stamped on the back. A seat on the county commission would have been much more befitting him than a seat in the county jail cell, or so it appeared to me.

The door slammed shut again. Now, it was only George and me, trapped in the vault together alone! He sat there silent, looking at me with the sad, pitiful expression of an innocent, helpless child who'd been unspeakably and outrageously violated and abused.

"I've forgiven them," with tears in his eyes.

My heart went out to him, and then I remembered John's words, "Don't let him pull you into his trap."

I began to understand how Ms. Moody, the professional counselor, after being duped by George, could possibly need counseling herself!

George Culhane was born with 20/20 vision, yet he spent his Earthly life totally blind to compassion and empathy for other human beings. He had the genius, savvy, and moves of a merciless predator eagle, yet no moral restraints.

I came to learn that George was totally self-focused. His life was a charade. He was a master of manipulation and control. But just as every lie is eventually exposed, a year after our visit in that cell, George's charade ended in the wee hours of Thursday morning May 24, 2007, when he put his head at the end of a 12-gauge shotgun barrel and pulled the trigger! He was 68.

George's next-to-last act of defiance was to curse the judge's restraining order and cross the Alabama state line. A day earlier, he had cut the court-ordered transmitter from his ankle.

He had been ARMED AND DANGEROUS! He had a shotgun, shells, and a gallon of Jack Daniels Whiskey, with a fourth of it running through his veins. He had a heart full of vengeance and hatred, but George was making his way home. The hell he put his family through became more intense as the years went by. Now his plan

## He Put Sue Aside

was to follow through on his threats of murdering his family before committing suicide.

Years earlier, although it seems like yesterday, Sue Hill was 15, beautiful, innocent, and pure as the driven snow. George was 18. As soon as Sue saw him, she was mesmerized, swept off her feet. He was so handsome, so witty, so smart, tall, muscular, wavy blond hair and sparkling blue eyes; young, Prince Charming in blue jeans with a country-boy, North Carolina drawl.

"He made me feel like I could fly!" she later said.

With no resistance or reservation, young Sue gave herself to George. She was 18 when they eloped and officially married.

Sue worked to help pay George's way to school. But George was out of place in the classroom: too much structure, accountability, and time spent looking up toward a professor who was an authority figure. Nobody was going to tell George what to do. He despised authority, and the classroom wasn't a suitable place for him to manipulate and take control, so he soon dropped out.

George's insanity continued to intensify. He saw Sue as his possession, a slave, a puppet, anything but a wife. George was a predator. Sue was his prey. In spite of the hell he put her through, Sue continued to love George. She held on to an idealistic thread of hope that somehow, some way, some day, he would change and become the husband and father he promised her that he would be.

All she ever wanted in life was to be a faithful wife and mother. He became the father of her two children, Jake and Katie.

For years, Sue lived in survival mode. Like a mother hen with impending danger circling overhead, she covered her little ones, ready at any time to give her own life to protect them. The bruises and scars marking her body were hidden. She wore long sleeves even in the summer, and never shorts or short dresses. The black eye?

"Oh, I was playing ball with Jake in the backyard, and I tripped!" she'd laugh and tell her friends—and then quickly change the subject.

They believed her story! Everybody loved George. He was much too nice, considerate, and likable to do anything like that! After all, he was Prince Charming!

Why didn't Sue pack up and leave? Because she was terrified of George, and he had her completely convinced that she and her children could not survive without him!

"He would continually mock me!" she recalls. He'd look at her, shake his head, and say, "Look at those fat legs! Your fat face! You're pathetic!"

"He broke me, and I became his puppet," she remembers.

Sue was his puppet, indeed, but not totally. She surrendered everything to him with two exceptions: little Jake and Katie. She was not about to turn them over to the predator. Her mission in life was to see that they were provided for and protected.

Sue also knew George's threats to harm the children were not idle threats, and she also knew that if she ran away, he would find them! His unbridled, insane abuse continued.

George had a number of lady friends, but the mistress he came to love most was named Miller: Miller High Life! At about the age of 21, he left the High Life. Beer no longer satisfied him. He fell in love with the hard stuff: *101 proof Kentucky Bourbon Whiskey.* The insanity and abuse went into overdrive!

Prince Charming became totally consumed and controlled by the *"prince of the power of the air, spiritual wickedness in the heavenly places."* The one we read about in **Ephesians 2:2.**

George was a genius of sorts. Just after he and Sue were married, he began working as a dispatcher for an asphalt construction company and, with one promotion after another, worked his way to the top.

# He Put Sue Aside

He had an astute ability to subtly "sow seeds of discord" among other employees, turning them against each other to his own advantage. That, along with his personal charm, the after-hours cocktail parties with "corporate brass," allowed George, the functional alcoholic, to move up fast.

As his power base increased, he became ruthless in corporate politics. He would surround himself with hard-working, competent employees who were totally loyal to him, and he'd gladly take credit for their accomplishments! Those who showed any signs of disloyalty were fired, oftentimes with fabricated charges.

Whenever a labor union would attempt to move in, George would be called. His success in brainwashing employees and keeping unions out obviously made him a favorite among the high-level executives.

George became division president and was in demand as a conference speaker, recognized as a national authority on asphalt construction. He remained with the same company for 35 years, and then his kingdom collapsed. Caught lying, stealing, and drunk, he was demoted and transferred to another state. He remained there 4 months, and then he was exposed and fired again.

Sue later found out that George had been a thief since childhood. Everywhere he went, he would steal just for the sake of stealing.

After being demoted and fired, he charmed his way into employment with five different companies within one year! Hired then fired! The lying, stealing, and drinking had become so much a part of him that he couldn't stop, nor did he want to!

Why was he fired but never prosecuted? He had the talent and skills of an Academy Award-winning actor! That's why! He'd have you feeling sorry for him and eating out of his hand in no time!

By 1995, the kids were grown and on their own. Jake graduated from college, married, and started his own family. Katie also graduated. Sue was so relieved. The children were finally able to make it on their own.

She ran away from George, but he hired a private investigator and found her. She wanted to believe more false promises and took him back.

The same, repeated scenario. The alcohol poured in. The demons came out. The abuse started again. Sue left again and took out a restraining order.

He called and left voice-mail messages threatening to kill her and the kids. He then showed up at her apartment, drunk and angry. She called the police, and he was arrested for violation of the order. The recorded threatening messages prevented him from masquerading and manipulating his way out of it. He was no longer a respected retired engineer but a Calhoun County Jail inmate.

Thankfully, afterward, before he made his way to Sue or the kids, he took his own life.

At OFA, we're learning to be very prayerful and careful about who we bring into the family. There are people in this world who will not be redeemed! Some are wolves and will remain wolves. There are those who need to be kept isolated from society all of their Earthly lives. Thank God some of them are! And thank God for our law-enforcement and judicial systems!

We live in the midst of a spiritual war, and the enemy is all around us, stalking us and our loved ones! We read about "the roaring lion seeking who he may devour" in **1 Peter 5:8.** To allow the enemy into our home without divine guidance and protection is to sacrifice the sheep! And we must prayerfully be "sober and on the alert"!

There are rare occasions when we are led to bring someone in knowing it will mean trouble. We're reminded of Judas Iscariot. He was brought into the family of disciples, our Lord knowing that Satan would enter him and the betrayal would come.

## He Put Sue Aside

Our Lord, Who is our example, did not cast the devil out of Judas! He washed his feet and called him "friend," and He tells us to be willing to do likewise! **John 13:15**

We're learning that God's purpose is being served even by the devil himself, but I did not want the inconvenience, emotional turmoil, stress, and danger! I did not want to allow George to come, but I sensed it was our Lord's leading, so I did anyway! Ours is not to question but to obey!

Back then, we welcomed George Culhane into our family with open arms, expecting a miracle! But, oftentimes, the miracle doesn't come the way we expect it!

Sue phoned me and began to ask all kinds of questions. I invited her to our Sunday afternoon, open-to-the-public meeting and was delighted to meet her in person when she arrived.

There she sat, next to George, in the front row, hanging on every word that was being shared! I had no idea that George had put her through so much for so many years!

I just knew that even though he was sick, she still loved him, and though I did not trust him, I was commanded to love him. So, I did!

All of us fell in love with Sue. She continued to come each week, sit next to George in the front row, and, so, naturally became a part of our family.

One Sunday following the meeting, Sue had just left; George approached me, crying. "Bob, you were so right! You said if I would 'let go and let God,' then healing would come. My family would be restored. It's happening, Bob! Just like you said! Thank you! Thank you!"

Later that afternoon, I discovered that he had been calling her, continuing the verbal abuse, threats, and harassment. I realized at that point that he was not going to cooperate, and it was time for him to go.

"Bob, please don't have me sent back to jail. That place is hell. I'll do whatever you say!"

It was too late. The deputies were on their way to arrest him! After several more months of incarceration, the judge then agreed for George to be released under the condition that he would wear an ankle transmitter and never enter the state. He said that he would comply, but he lied again.

As soon as we received word of his death, I phoned Sue. She asked that the memorial service be held outdoors at Our Father's Arms for just the family before it was announced publicly.

She asked that I bring my guitar, and "please keep it informal. Wear jeans and T-shirt, like you usually do," she said.

George's memorial service was a time for closure. The family was together. We were all encouraged to, by our Lord's grace, "Forgive and Let go."

While George was incarcerated, one of the grandchildren asked, "Where's Papa?"

Another said, "Papa's not here because he is sick."

Simple enough for a child and so true.

Papa was a sick man, and, in the eyes of divine reason, mental and emotional illness is no different than physical illness. Forgiveness is always in order.

"Father, forgive them. They know not what they do" **Luke 23:34** and "Let those of you without sin cast the first stone." **John 8:7**

A loved one who is mentally ill remains a loved one. Years of abuse, hostility, and even the taking of one's own life can typically cause those who remain to keep questioning why and become mentally and emotionally ill themselves.

We are left struggling with the futility of what we could have done different to avert the tragedy. Vacillating from blaming themselves, to blaming the deceased loved one, reoccurring nightmares, all manner of guilt, regret, confusion, haunted by trying to relive the past and make it different.

After all Sue had been through, she continues to defy the expected, normal psychological profile. She is healthy, happy, productive, and a delight to be with. Sue loves our Lord and is filled with His hope. Sue loves life.

For a number of years now, she has been actively involved in jail ministry, working alongside Chaplain Richard at the County Jail, showing personal interest and care for the inmates. She also calls and ministers to their families. She enjoys and delights in her children and grandchildren, and is such a powerful example of how the grace of our Lord Jesus will empower one to let go of the past, forgive, and continue to learn to live the freedom of unfailing love!

## A Way with Words

*Darkness all around.*
*I can hear the sound of a world filled with hate.*
*No sane way to escape.*
*So why bother?*
*A little child lost from home,*
*Afraid and all alone.*
*That is until she hears the voice of her Father.*

*Away with Words*
*To a place called Paradise.*
*Away with Words,*

## Learning to Love a Porcupine

*Words of love and life.*
*He's taking us Away with Words*
*From this world of sin and strife,*
*From this world filled with lies,*
*From this world that dies.*
*Jesus has A Way with Words.*

*Such a sweet sound we hear.*
*God Himself is drawing near.*
*Giving us ears to hear.*
*He's taking us home.*
*In the darkness he speaks so clear.*
*His words erase all doubt and fear,*
*Healing hearts and drying hopeless tears.*
*The child's no longer alone.*

# CHAPTER 23

## The Revelation of Resurrection

FEAR anticipates destruction. (**Job 3:25**) Faith anticipates redemption! (**Matthew 21:22**) Satan, the father of lies (**John 8:44**) has no power within himself. (**Colossians 2:15** NLT) He must have the cooperation of human beings to do his stealing, killing, and destroying (**1 Peter 5:8**). This deception and cooperation is facilitated through Fear! *Fear is faith in the devil, the father of lies!*

Unfailing FAITH is activated, energized, and expressed by unfailing LOVE. (**Galatians 5:6b** Amp) As one receives the Perfect Love appropriated and transmitted through the innocent God-man's blood-soaked Cross, Jesus then becomes the Author and Perfecter of one's **FAITH**: **F**inding the **A**wesome **I**nvisible **T**ruth of **H**eaven! (**Hebrews 11:2**)

Faith in the lie (fear) must be fed. We are bombarded by fear through the media and every other conceivable outlet. The consequence is: misery and torment evidenced by complaining, criticizing, blame shifting, whining, scoffing, murmuring, and backbiting, always feeling threatened.

We never realize that we are in a demonic prayer meeting, giving credibility and power to the lie, the lie that says we're not loved with a perfect love that never fails and "casts out fear!" **1 John 4:18** That is until . . .

The **REVELATION OF RESURRECTION** happens! We begin to awaken and start feeding on the Word of Truth and the reality of His perfect Love that is not affected by anyone's opinion or behavior! **(Romans 8:38, 39)**

As one is birthed into this awareness of truth, freedom is the result. The complaining begins to decrease, and gratitude begins to increase.

That's when the redemptive miracles multiply all around whoever will receive! That's when one learns to anticipate redemption rather than destruction in every adverse situation. Faith it, not fear it!

## Eddie

When Eddie was seven, he came to his dad one evening, desiring to be saved. His dad prayed with him, and, the next Sunday, he made his decision public and was baptized.

His good nature, compassion, and love for people, particularly the disadvantaged, turned him into a fun-loving, devil-may-care party animal! He had no idea the seduction would begin with one, carefree drink of one beer.

The government-endorsed and -promoted billion-dollar industry in America and prevalent drug of choice, alcohol can sedate the conscience, setting one up to engage in behavior that's totally destructive and out of character! *That's not true for all, but for so many!*

Eddie gradually became one of those who fall for the lie that you have to get high to enjoy life!

# The Revelation of Resurrection

Like the outlaws he associated with, he began to combine alcohol with opiates and any assortment of drugs, including crystal methamphetamine until he was consumed by the addiction—doing whatever it took to get the next fix!

His social group became renegade criminals and addicts! He never intended for it to happen. The seduction was slow and subtle. It was the lifestyle of people he had grown to love, care for, and identify with.

Where did the years go? By the time he was forty, his life of addiction and crime had him classified by the state as an habitual felon.

The road he was on always leads to death by overdose or prison. His family was so grateful that, for Eddie, it was the latter.

Handcuffs, legs chains, head shaved, white, used prison clothes, transported by armed guards to *"Bloody Bibb,"* one of the most violent prisons.

It would be there, if he lived, he would complete the remaining 18 months of his sentence. The guard was waiting at the gate with a "body release" form for him to sign, giving the state permission to dispose of his remains should it become necessary—as it oftentimes was!

After signing the form, the guard took his arm to escort him into the pit of demons. All the guard said was, ***"Welcome to Hell!"***

The Alabama prison violence made the national news: *"Understaffed prisons in Alabama are overflowing with inmates who are armed with makeshift weapons and will kill officers over food and will kill fellow inmates for any number of reasons.*

*Inmates are drugged, raped, and tortured for days at a time, sometimes in retaliation for reporting sexual abuse."*

These are the findings of a federal investigation of Alabama prisons, released in 2019 by the U.S. Department of Justice:

> *"Murder, as well as rape and torture, are very real threats for Alabama prison inmates, investigators found. The assaults are often committed by inmates with deadly, handmade weapons.*
>
> *Prisoners at Bibb said that "everyone" has knives, and prisoners need a weapon to stay alive. One prisoner stated that "Bibb is a place where you have to fight the day you arrive or you'll be a bitch, so you get you a knife."*

Seeing it on the news and reading articles like this is horrible enough, but what if it's your own son locked up in there?

Eddie's family remained at home feeling helpless. How did this nightmare happen?

Wondering where they went wrong. Tormented by hopeless, irrelevant blame shifting, sleepless nights—that is, until the **REVELATION OF RESURRECTION!**

The warfare is real, but it's not a fight with the wayward son, the prison officials, the politicians, the system, or the drug dealers. The fight is not with sin, the flesh, or demons. The real fight is the **1 Timothy 6:12, FIGHT OF FAITH!**

The prayer of faith moves the hand of Almighty God, and there are no greater words of faith than THANK YOU! **Philippians 4:6,7** is the key out of anxiety and fear!

All fear is the fear of losing something! Anything one is afraid of losing is another god before God. The prayer of fear is a prayer asking God to cooperate with one's idolatry!

Had Eddie and his recovery been his family's passion, preoccupation, purpose, and obsession, then, as it has with so many others, fear would have destroyed them all! To pray effectively we can have NO OTHER GODS BEFORE HIM!

## The Revelation of Resurrection

How do you do that? How does one become a disciple and have a "disregard for father, mother, brother, sister, son, and daughter in comparison to a love for Christ as we're told to do in **Luke 14:26–33?** The answer is simply, *WE CAN'T!*

We are powerless! *Only God can do it in whosoever is willing for Him to!* All you and I can do is to very personally bring our willingness to Him! Jesus does the rest!

It's then that one's perspective changes! One begins to see everything and everyone, including all loved ones, as belonging to the Lord! One no longer tries to possess that which is not his or hers to possess! Finally catching on to letting go!

Eddie hit reality head on in the over-crowded hell of Bloody Bibb! Drugs were smuggled in and readily available to anyone who would sell their body and soul for them. Eddie remained clean and sober and began to see clearly, without the veil of intoxication, what drugs to do people.

Fault-finding and blame-shifting only feeds hopelessness. Eddie was caught in a trap he never saw coming! His out-of-character behavior had no effect on our Lord Jesus Christ's faithfulness and claim on his life.

Albert Einstein is quoted as saying, *"Tragedy introduces a man to himself!"* Eddie met himself in the tragic Hell of Bloody Bibb!

In daily contact with his dad by phone, he became the point man for OFA ministry to other inmates, many who had no outside family support; books, study Bibles (*some in Spanish*) shoes, and basic necessities were channeled to the socially unacceptable outcasts that Eddie continued to have compassion for, but this time, he was there to help them live, not enable them to die in addiction and for him to die with them!

Surrounded in a den of demons, Eddie had no weapon or knife, yet he was sober, without fear, and, therefore, respected even by psychopath killers who were packed like sardines in an overcrowded, bolted down, padlocked, no-escaping metal warehouse.

The 24/7 clanging echoes, screams, and overlapping noises of hate-filled men, the constant wind of giant fans trying to keep the heat index down, would eat away at the nerves and eventually drive anyone insane, if they weren't already! Tormented souls living and sleeping all around him! *Again, he had no fear!*

Eddie was protected during his time in hell, released, and, as of this writing, has been living and helping in the OFA home of reentry. He's doing contract work and is now on staff with OFA, leading in the further development of OFA Prison Ministry and Reentry.

Those who get knocked down and keep getting back up are the true heroes in this life! Eddie, like the rest of us, remains a work in progress, learning to live the overcoming life, fulfilling his call and destiny.

The large painting by Briton Riviere, from 1872, hangs on the wall in the prayer room at OFA. Instead of "Daniel in the Lion's Den" we now call it: Eddie in Bloody Bibb!

**Eddie at Bloody Bibb**

## The Revelation of Resurrection

# Afraid of Faith

*So many for so long*
*Have been walking along the beaten path.*
*Trembling hands holding trembling hands*
*Afraid to take their heads from the sand,*
*Slaves to what they think they understand,*
*Afraid of Faith, Afraid of Faith*

*Paralyzed by fear and regret,*
*Trying so hard to forget,*
*Babel fell, and hell is not full yet.*
*Afraid of Faith, Afraid of Faith*

*Perfect love cast out fear.*
*Perfect love is standing here.*
*I receive You, now I'm safe.*
*How could I ever be, ever be Afraid of Faith*

## CHAPTER 24

## Thank You Therapy

Billy was born fragile. By the time he was 18 months old, he kept wheezing, suffering coughing, nose running, fever, apnea (short periods without breathing) listlessness, and frightening contractions in his chest wall. He started turning blue around the lips. His parents rushed him to the hospital. He was admitted. The diagnosis was respiratory syncytial virus (RSV). The heavy doses of antibiotics and breathing treatments seemed to be effective, but there was always the concern that his lungs would not hold up.

In his seventh year, he began to feel his need for a Savior. He called his grandad, a pastor, aside one afternoon. "Papa, I want to be saved," was all he said.

His Papa simply shared with him, "God so loves you, Billy, that He gave His only begotten, innocent Son to take the consequences of our sin upon Himself, and if you will simply receive His forgiveness, trust, rely upon Him, and surrender your life to Him, then you, too, will be saved."

Billy simply gave an affirming nod and prayed the sinner's prayer. His Papa had the privilege of baptizing him a few days later in their little country Baptist Church.

Billy continued to grow and develop with no known problems until he was 13. Late one night he suddenly woke up in a panic! He couldn't breathe!

His family began making plans to get him to a specialist. A few days later, it happened again! His family was praying and frantically searching for answers and what direction to take!

Billy has always been a very private person. He's sociable but at the same time likes being alone. He "keeps his cards close to his chest," so to speak.

His Papa stopped by his room to visit with him the day after his second panic attack.

"Billy, tell me about what's been happening to you. You wake up and can't breathe?"

He nodded in obvious anxiety.

"Do you think you're going to suffocate and die?"

The fear in his face, the tear in his eye made it obvious that this young man was in a dark, personal nightmare! He simply nodded again.

"Billy, hand me your Bible. I want to show you something. Here in **1 John 4:18** we read that fear involves torment! Fear could very well be the cause of your panic attacks! In that same verse, we read the solution and how to go free: 'Perfect love casts out fear.'

"As you well remember, all those years ago as a young boy, you received the Lord Jesus Christ into your heart, and He has not left you! Let's look at **Colossians 1:27**. He continues to live "in you." Everyone else may be asleep in the middle of the night, but He is not. He's there with you! Even inside of you!

## Thank You Therapy

"**Philippians 4:6,7** gives us the key to overcoming anxiety! It's 'prayer with THANKSGIVING!' And how well you know **Psalm 23!**

"If that ever happens to you again, start thanking Jesus for being your Savior Who leads you beside still waters, Who makes you to lie down in green pastures, Who restores your soul, Who prepares a table before you in the presence of your enemies, Who even walks with you through the Valley of the Shadow of Death.

"Start thanking Him—His Word says that His peace that passes all understanding will guard your heart and mind. Keep thanking Him for His perfect love that casts out fear! And see what happens! Will you do that?"

He simply smiled and nodded again! Papa prayed a simple prayer, thanking our Lord for taking care of His son, Billy, and off he went!

A week later, in passing, Papa asked him, "Billy, has that happened to you again?"

He smiled and nodded again.

"How many times?"

He held up one finger and simply said, "Once."

No more tormenting nightmares! **Thank You Therapy works!!!!!!**

That's not all! Billy started running and running and running like Forrest Gump! He graduated from high school with honors. His athletic achievements in Track and Field, Baseball, and Wrestling are quite impressive, but get this: That kid who couldn't breathe was All State Cross Country, leading his team to win the state championship!

Surrounded by thousands at the State Cross Country meet, Papa had to do a double take when he noticed something written on the calves of Billy's legs. During the warm-up, he moved in to get a closer look. Billy had taken a black felt pen and wrote on his left calf "**Psalm 23.**" On the other, "**Phil. 4:5,6!**"

Following the State Championship, he signed a scholarship to run Cross Country at Jacksonville State University!

That ain't bad for a kid who couldn't breathe! Thank You Therapy Works!

Billy, All State Cross Country

## Two Words

*We're going to be "out of here"*
*A lot longer than we're "in here."*
*As long as we are "in here"*
*It's but by a breath.*
*We're going to be "out of here"*
*A lot longer than we're "in here."*
*Fear not—why not enjoy the time you've got left?*
*As easy as Two Words*
*As easy as Two Words*

## Thank You Therapy

*Jesus, thank you, Jesus.*
*Thank you for Your love that never fails.*
*Jesus, thank you, Jesus.*
*Thank You for Your love that will prevail!*
*Thank You for being our dearest friend.*
*Thank You for Your love that never ends.*

# CHAPTER 25

## The Light Shined on Me

It was about 2003 that I accepted a collect call from the Calhoun County jail. The young lady was frantic and desperate. She was crying and pleading for help.

"Mr. McLeod, my name is Christie! My brothers went to school with your son. I'm not a bad person. Please help. My Daddy has a disease and is paralyzed. My mother needs me to help with him. They don't have enough money to buy his medicine. I need to work and help them! Please help us! I'll do anything! I promise! Just help me get out! Please, sir!"

"How old are you, Christie?" I interrupted.

"Twenty-six! Please help us! I won't let you down! I promise!"

"What are you locked up for, Christie?"

There was a pause, and then she sheepishly replied,

"Crystal meth. I got in with the wrong crowd, but I'm really not a bad person!"

I shared with Christie that our Lord Jesus loves her so much that He went through the suffering and death on a cross and has forgiven her all of her sins. I prayed with her and assured her that we would continue to pray and help in any way as He leads.

I then phoned her mom and verified Christie's story. Several days later, I contacted the Calhoun County District Attorney's office. Upon the DA's recommendation, Christie was court ordered to our care for six months.

Patti and I went to the jail and brought Christie to her home. She became like a daughter to us. She moved in with her parents, got a part-time job in a local grocery store, and attended all of our meetings.

She prayed to receive Jesus and was baptized. We embraced her family and held several of our Tuesday-evening Bible studies in their home next to her dad's bed as he helplessly lay there, connected to a feeding tube and breathing machine. He was suffering with Guillain-Barre Syndrome. We asked the Lord to heal him.

A week before her six months were completed, Christie disappeared. I notified the DA, and warrants were issued. We began praying that Christie would be caught and arrested. It took about four months.

When she was arrested, a drug-induced toxic psychosis had her in such a rage that she had to be placed in an isolated cell. Several weeks later, she called me.

"Bob, this is Christie. I'm in jail. Can you come see me?"

"I know you're in jail. We prayed you'd get arrested! Praise God! How did you call me without it being collect?"

"I'm out back washing police cars, and they let me use their phone. Can you come see me?"

"Christie, I'm only a couple of blocks away. Can I come now?"

"Just a minute."

I heard her ask the police, "Can he come now?"

"Yes! They said it's okay!"

## The Light Shined on Me

I just happened to be one block away!

"I'll be there in five minutes!'

When I arrived, the officers led me to a private visitor's area, and Christie walked in.

After a hug and tears, she said, "I'm so sorry I disappointed you and Patti! After all you've done for me, I was so wrong. I'll make it up to you somehow. I'm so sorry!"

"Christie, that's enough of that! You haven't disappointed us in the least! We haven't missed a meal or good night's sleep worrying about you! You see, our love for you has no expectations! We're just grateful you're okay! We've never stopped praying for you—faith, not fear!"

I then shared with her the Parable of the Prodigal son, in her case "daughter," in **Luke 15**! Another hug, more tears, and I was on my way.

"We'll stay in close touch as our Lord continues to make a way for you!"

Christie's jail cell became a ministry center for other young ladies who were arrested. There Christie shared the love of Jesus, read the Bible, and prayed with prostitutes, drug addicts, thieves, etc. Satan's attack is indeed God's opportunity!

Several months later, I went to court with Christie. The judge had become a dear friend over the years and one who respects and trusts the ministry and work of OFA. After a severe threat and reprimand, the judge re-released Christie to our care.

We were able to provide Christie with a partial scholarship and also help her mom and dad. She finished top of her class and is now a practicing registered nurse. She's married and a mother of four.

I was privileged to conduct her wedding ceremony a few years ago, and one of the most unforgettable highlights of my life was seeing Christie's dad, trembling and feeble, leaning on his cane, with an unflinching determination. Slowly, he walked his precious daughter down the aisle to be joined with her husband!

Christie's own words: "I found my way out of darkness. The Light shined for me!"

I asked Christie when the light shined on her.

"When you came to see me in jail that day and told me that you and Patti were not disappointed in me. That's when it happened! I then realized for the first time that God is not disappointed in me, either! He does not condemn me! His love for me has no expectations. He loves me just like I am."

## Stop Wasting Our Time

*My heart's been broken*
*By the burden of betraying*
*The only One Who ever loved me enough to die.*
*I know I'm so undeserving,*
*Each time I try to serve Him,*
*I fall so far behind until I cry,*
*"Jesus, why would You even offer me the time of day?*
*You've got every reason to leave me here,*
*Go Your own way.*
*I know I deserve Your judgment, Lord*
*For being so untrue."*
*and then He smiles, says, "Come here, child.*
*No matter what you do,*
*You'll never keep me from loving you."*

## The Light Shined on Me

*I even tried to talk Him out of loving me,*
*But He just wouldn't listen,*
*Wouldn't pay me no mind.*
*I even tried to talk Him out of loving me.*
*He said,*
*"Child, Stop Wasting Our Time."*

*Now, what are you going to do with a love like that?*
*Lord, into your arms I fall.*
*Suffering love held nothing back.*
*Take this wretched soul, my God,*
*I surrender all!*

## CHAPTER 26

## USA Gang

I vaguely remember, as a young toddler, snuggling up next to my grandmother, sitting on an old, hard wooden church pew on a hot summer Sunday morning. The faithful few in that little frame country church house depended on a cross breeze coming through the raised windows to help endure or even survive the heat. Air conditioning wasn't heard of yet. I suspect that there were a lot more sermons about Hell in those days.

I can still faintly smell her perfume. I can feel her one arm around me, holding me close; with the other, she would wave a flat, wooden handle that looked like a giant popsicle stick, stapled to a cardboard fan with a picture of Jesus and some angels painted on it.

I'm reminded of the soft, rhythmic, consistent breeze, as she'd keep time with the hymns they were singing, determined to keep me cool. That breeze felt so good! I sure do miss that precious lady we called "Momma Dee Dee."

## Learning to Love a Porcupine

As she would fan, her daughter, my momma, would pound the keys on that old, out-of-tune, spinet piano. My daddy, with an open hymn book in one hand, the other hand waving as if he was directing the Mormon Tabernacle Choir, would lead the handful of saints in singing the sacred hymns that were, without me even suspecting, becoming engraved into my subconscious soul for life!

Down through the years, laughter, and tears of life's journey, I have on occasion, found myself in some of the most unusual, unpredictable, even life-threatening places, and each time, without exception, there's one particular hymn that keeps coming back, faintly echoing in my mind:

*"I can hear my Savior calling, I can hear my Savior calling, I can hear my Savior calling, 'Take thy cross and follow, follow Me.' Where He leads me, I will follow. Where He leads me, I will follow. Where He leads me, I will follow. I'll go with Him, with Him, all the way."*

This hymn was written in 1890 by Ernest Blandy, a Salvation Army officer just before he left a comfortable position in a well-established church for a New York City waterfront slum called *"Hell's Kitchen."*

A dear mentor and friend of years past put it like this: "When you follow Jesus, you never know where you're gonna *"pop up!"*

**Bob with gang members at Pollsmore Prison**

## USA Gang

Some years ago, I *"popped up"* and spent the best part of a day in another *Hell's Kitchen*, a cell block in the Pollsmore Maximum Security Prison in Cape Town, South Africa, surrounded by young inmates who were gang members awaiting court dates.

This part of the prison must have been constructed in the 19th century. The cell was old, musty, mildewed, in terrible disrepair. There were probably 50 or 60 young men crammed into a space large enough for only half that many. Bunks with filthy sheets and blankets lined the stained, faded brick walls.

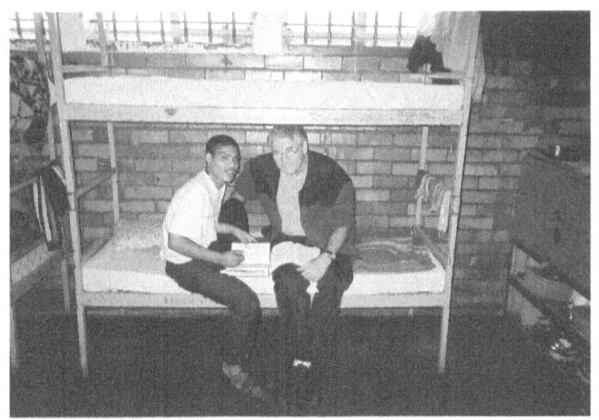

**Bob with Reginald in Bible Study**

At the far end, out in the open, was a nasty, leaking, covered in mold, stained stainless steel toilet! That cell had a God-awful stench. It was a filthy, roach-infested cage, a nightmare!

The young inmates were confined to that horrible place for 23 1/2 hours a day! When they heard the hollow echoes of a guard walking down the hallway to unlock the massive chain that sealed the six-inch-thick, steel door, there would literally be a stampede!

They were allowed 30 minutes to walk in the courtyard under the watchful eyes of guards armed with AK-47s. 30 minutes! That was it!

Then, like cattle, they were herded back to the cell. Some of them had been there for two or three years awaiting their day in court!

The presence of a white man with a southern drawl and 12-string guitar was a novelty to them. They were overly friendly at first, but, after a few songs sharing the love of our Lord, I began to sense a more genuine openness, and in one young man in particular.

His name is Reginald. He had been in a gang fight, shot point blank range in the head. How he survived with his mental faculties intact is a miracle. With a small, worn, opened Bible held six inches from his one good eye, pen in hand, he attentively held on to every word I shared with him.

He led me to his bunk. We were there, having a personal Bible study, **15th Chapter, Gospel of John.** The Word was coming alive for both of us!

Then we heard the guard approaching. The stampede began.

"Go ahead, Reginald. We'll continue after the break."

Like a sheep dying of thirst finding water, he sharply replied, "Oh, no! Let's keep going!"

An hour or so later, my armed escort arrived. I hated to leave Reginald, but my time was up.

"Reginald, what is that tattoo on your arm?" I asked as I was getting up to leave.

I had noticed the same tattoo on some of the others. It was simply the letters, "USA."

"Bob, it's the gang! The USA Gang!" he said, somewhat startled, dropping his head in shame as soon as I asked.

"It's the most feared gang in Cape Town, Bob! Cold-blooded, random murder of an innocent person is part of the initiation!"

## USA Gang

"What does 'USA' stand for?"

"Don't you know?" he asked, shocked at my question.

"It's your country, Bob, the United States of America! The gangs down here respect and admire the violence of your country!"

That was a heartbreaking revelation to me. After returning to the familiar, comfortable surroundings of home, I couldn't help but weep, realizing that we are being destroyed, sheep led to slaughter, oblivious to what's really going on, even in our churches!

So often, in ignorance, we are manipulated into joining a social club with a steeple on top, count ourselves, entertain ourselves, blind to the fact that our feel-good, boastful pride of life, self-centered "Give me" gospel has no power! Oftentimes there are **Matthew 24:24** counterfeits that add to the deception.

It's so simple a child can see it: When it's "man centered," not "Christ centered," there will never be authentic, life-transforming power and protection!

**2 Timothy 4:6**: "For a time is coming when people will no longer listen to sound and wholesome teaching. They will follow their own desires and will look for teachers who will tell them whatever their itching ears want to hear."

**2 Timothy 3:5**: ". . . holding to a form of godliness, although they have denied its power . . ."

There's that hymn again! *"Where He leads me, I will follow."*

Or, am I singing the hymn as I continue to do just as I please and pretend, assuming that He is following me!

**Ephesians 5:14**: "Therefore he says, awake you that sleep, and arise from the dead, and Christ shall give you light."

On my way back to our precious homeland, the United States of America, these song lyrics came to me:

Learning to Love a Porcupine

# We Dig Our Own Grave

26 years old, he stares at the wall
In the nursing home
No one's home at all.
The drugs took his mind,
We pray not his soul.
Can he be saved?
He dug his own grave.

"From the time that they're born
We fill them with hate,
Through the TV shows, the videos,
And the movies they rate.
Tune to violent cartoons and it's a fool
Who wonders why, there's murder in our schools!

We Dig Our Own Grave!
We dig them deep!
We Dig Our Own Grave
As Heaven weeps!
We must be so depraved.
We just keep on digging our own grave!"

He came for His own, yet He was despised.
They could not see, He was God in disguise.
We nailed Him to a cross.
He died,

*But He came out of that grave!*
*Now He's alive and mighty to save*

*Those who Dig Their Own Grave.*
*We dug them deep!*
*We Dug Our Own Grave but*
*Heaven had a promise to keep!*
*By His grace we are saved!*
*No longer digging our own grave!!!!"*

## CHAPTER 27

## Holman Prison Death Row

Michael Donald, only 19, had been beaten savagely, his throat had been slashed, and "his blue jeans and blue jean jacket were covered in dirt and dried blood."

A cross was burned on the lawn of the Mobile, Alabama, courthouse a few hours before Donald's body was discovered. The murder took place March 20, 1981.

One of his killers was Henry Frances Hays, who was then 26 years old. For the crime, Henry was executed in the Alabama Electric Chair, June 6, 1997. Before he died, Henry and I first met in 1990. He was an inmate on death row, Holman Prison in Atmore, Alabama.

Even though it was a 10-hour drive round trip, I set aside one day each month to go down for a visit. Since the visits lasted four or five hours, by the time I got home, it sure did make for a long day! I was much younger, then!

Why did I leave my business and family to go spend time with rapists, thieves, murderers, and the worst of criminals?

## Learning to Love a Porcupine

Death Row, Holman Prison

Henry Hays

It sure didn't make for wise financial planning! With my one-man business in a home office at that time, I was able to provide for my family and keep the bills paid, but we typically had nothing extra left and lived month to month. Why did I do that?

Why did I start taking in outcasts and risking the safety of my family? Why did OFA even happen? Why would anyone in their right mind spend so much time with people who are considered losers, some dangerous and most without a penny to their name?

I've tried, but I never have been able to logically answer that question or justify my life's choice. A couple of years ago, a film company came in to produce a documentary of Our Father's Arms and Dugger Mountain Music Hall.

My precious wife, Patti, was interviewed and asked the simple question: "Why does your husband do this?" Her answer caught me a bit by surprise. She shrugged her shoulders, shook her head in resolve, and simply said: *"It's just in him."*

That moment settled it for me. No sense in trying to explain, justify, or figure it out. It's simply who I was born to be. Can't help it! I was born with the, *"Heart Bigger Than Head"* disorder!

So there! That's that! No more wasting time trying to analyze or justify. Times runnin' short. Let's get on with livin' it!

## Holman Prison Death Row

Back to Death Row:

I was tempted to hate Henry Hays for what he had done, but I grew to love him. We'd visit with no interruptions and for however long he was comfortable. He soon realized that I really did care about him, with no hidden agenda.

Rev. Williams, a black Pentecostal preacher who lived in Montgomery, would on occasion go down to Atmore with me. He's the one who introduced me to Henry.

Rev. Williams had earlier prayed with Henry to receive our Lord. How ironic! A black man praying with KKK racists who hated black people so much that he'd kill in cold blood!

I was able to get past the headlines and court records, and hear the "rest of the story."

Like many young men, Henry's dad was his hero! His name was Bennie Jack Hays. He was a preacher and also the second highest-ranking Klansman in Alabama.

Henry was indoctrinated and brainwashed into believing that black skin was God's curse on the lineage of Ham for rebellion against his father, Noah. The account in **Genesis 9** has been wrongly used down through the centuries to justify man's inhumanity against man and horrible cruelty against ethnic groups and even slavery.

Henry was taught well and was being groomed to carry on his family's legacy of hate, using the Holy Bible to do it! He had even become a preacher himself!

"I had no clue how wrong we were! I honestly thought my dad was a man of God, and I honestly thought God was on our side!" he told me with tears in his eyes. "I'm so sorry!"

Back to Michael Donald: He was the youngest of his Mother Beulah Mae's six children. He was her baby boy!

Mrs. Beulah Mae Donald

After being sentenced to the electric chair, the judge asked Henry if he had anything to say for killing Michael. He sheepishly looked up toward Mrs. Donald, crying almost uncontrollably, and, with a trembling, broken voice, whispered to her, "I'm so sorry. Please forgive me."

*"Young man", she said, "the Lord Jesus Christ forgave each and every one of us from a bloody cross that day; and I forgave you as soon as I heard it happen and before I even knew yo' name, because my Lord says for me to."*

Upon first hearing of her baby boy being savagely murdered, a grieving mother might isolate herself in torment, hopeless pity, personal horror, and heartbreak that no one could ever begin to imagine. She might have grieved privately and, if pressured enough by the news media, issue a brief statement of regret and sorrow, and then return to her victimized mourning.

But not Beulah Mae Donald! No! She wasn't about to settle for that! She insisted on an open casket for her battered son "so the world could

## Holman Prison Death Row

know." She challenged the silence of the Klan and the uncooperative attitude of the criminal justice system. She arrived early and was front row every moment of Henry's trial, staring the devil in the face! Yes!

Two convictions weren't enough for her. She didn't want revenge. She didn't want money. All she ever wanted, she says, was to prove that *"Michael did no wrong."*

Mrs. Donald's determination inspired a handful of lawyers and civil-rights advocates, black and white.

Early in 1984, Morris Dees, co-founder of the Southern Poverty Law Center, suggested that Mrs. Donald file a civil suit against the members of the United Klans of America.

The killers were, he believed, carrying out an organizational policy set by the group's Imperial Wizard. If Dees could prove in court that this *"theory of agency"* applied, the Klan would be as liable for the murder as a corporation is for the actions its employees take in the service of business.

Mrs. Donald agreed to participate in the civil suit. In February 1987, an all-white jury in Mobile, Alabama, needed to deliberate only four hours before awarding her seven million dollars.

In May, the Klan in Alabama turned over the deed to its only significant asset, the $225,000 national headquarters building in Tuscaloosa.

Meanwhile, Mrs. Donald's attorney moved to seize the property and garnish the wages of individual defendants.

*"Thank God, the Klan, at this point, is washed up,"* said Henry Hays to me from his cell on death row.

Mrs. Donald left this life September 18, 1988. She was 67 and died of natural causes.

Perhaps she, her son Michael, and Henry are resting in peace together, only by the shed blood of the innocent Lamb of God, our Lord Jesus Christ 2000 years ago! Mercy and Grace poured out for every man!

Is the Bible the inherent Word of Almighty God? Bennie Jack Hays and his family would defiantly say, "Yes!"

So would Westboro Baptist Church in Topeka, Kansas. You've seen them on the nightly news:

Westboro Baptist Church members picketing

This is from the Westboro Baptist Church web site 2017:

> *Established in 1955 by Pastor Fred Phelps, the Westboro Baptist Church (WBC) of Topeka, Kansas, still exists today as an Old School (or, Primitive) Baptist Church. We adhere to the teachings of the Bible, preach against all form of sin (e.g., fornication, adultery [including divorce and remarriage, sodomy), and insist that the sovereignty of God and the doctrines of grace be taught and expounded publicly to all men.*
>
> *Even though the Arminian lies that "God loves everyone" and "Jesus died for everyone" are being taught from nearly every pulpit in this generation, this hasn't always been the case. If you are in a church that supposedly believes the Bible, and you are hearing these lies, then your church doesn't teach what the Bible teaches.*
>
> *If you care about your never-dying soul, you will carefully read every word of this web site, along with the entire Bible."*

Am I a product of my family's worldview, like Henry Hays or Fred Phelps? Do I accept an interpretation of the Bible as the inherent Word of God, or do I reject the Bible altogether, because of the sick, ridiculous, destructive interpretations?

It's recorded in the Bible, **John 5:39** that Jesus said, "You study the Scriptures diligently because you think that in them you have eternal life. These are the very Scriptures that testify about Me."

Therefore, life is not to be found in knowing the Bible, but in knowing the God of the Bible!

How can you tell someone really knows the Lord?

"By their fruit you will recognize them". **Matthew 7:16**

**John 13:35** "By this everyone will know you are my disciples, if you love one another."

If your theology lines up with reality, it'll come out lookin' like: Lay-your-life-down, no-hook-in-it, forgiving **LOVE!** That's how you'll know!

Thank you, precious, sister, Beulah Mae Donald for letting the world see the real Jesus in you!

A pastor friend who is also a mental-health professional did his internship in a mental hospital in Mobile, Alabama. He told me the true story of a patient there. It inspired these song lyrics:

## *Unholy Lie*

*"In an insane asylum in a dark and lonely room*
*An old man cries, "Would somebody read me the*
   *Bible, please?"*
*The Chaplain walks right by him*
*Through the shadows and the gloom*

*And leaves the old man all alone
Pleading on his knees!
Jesus says in Matthew 5:29,
"If your eye causes you to stumble, gouge it out!"
The old man didn't doubt. He obeyed.
Now the light that God had given him,
He never again will see because there's only empty sockets
Where his eye use to be!
The doer of the Word is so alone and so afraid!*

*The One Who inspired the writing of the Bible
must inspire the reading of the Bible
or else your Holy Bible is an unholy lie!*

*The Bible-believing Pharisees
Searched the Scriptures daily,
sharpening their swords, ever ready to condemn.
When God Himself came to their town,
they gnashed their teeth and put Him down.
Raised their Bibles proudly high and cried, "Crucify Him!"*

## They Don't Know You

*His trembling fist would pound the pulpit
And his eyes shone like fire.
He'd gasp for breath as he strutted back 'n' forth.
Claimed he hated drunken bums 'n' liars.
He said the Lord and him had come to destroy sin,*

## Holman Prison Death Row

*Pass the plate 'fore the church goes broke.*
*Well, I got up and left when he scared his flock to death*
*Commenced to telling them how to vote!*

*We never do hear them mention*
*the joy and the peace*
*That comes when someone finds the truth.*
*We never do hear them mention*
*The Light that leads us home.*
*Oh Jesus, it's so obvious*
*They don't know you.*

*Under her arm she held a Bible,*
*In her hand a collection plate.*
*Standing out in front of the liquor Store*
*Motivated by contempt and hate.*
*She said, "You sinnin' fools,*
*You spent it on booze.*
*Let the Lord have what you got left."*
*But the Lord never got the conscience money.*
*She kept it and spent it on herself.*

*Religious competition, spiritual pride*
*Are tools that the devil loves to use.*
*Lord, it's no surprise when we stop to realize*
*It was religious folk who drove the nails in You.*
*After a day of selfish violence,*
*I hear Your voice pierce the deathly silence,*
*"Father, forgive them. They know not what they do."*

## CHAPTER 28

## One on One

"Billy, you're going to die."

What? Nobody wants to hear that, especially Billy!

A fun-loving eighteen year old with the prime of life just beginning and so many *"Roll Tide"* partying years ahead of him, was lying there in a bed in the UAB Pediatric Cancer Center in Birmingham, Alabama, with terror in his eyes! We loved Billy as if he were our own son.

The purpose of my visit was to try to bring comfort to Billy and his family, so when I heard myself say those words, I was at first shocked!

The doctor had said, "The chemo may save him."

I heard myself say, "Billy, you're going to die!"

Billy's mom, Dorothy, stood there heartbroken but somehow seemed to understand.

I heard myself continue, "Billy, you may live for what we think is a long time, or you may die today. No one knows! But one thing we do know for sure! Physical death is certain for everyone! Every one of us, sooner or later, must do private, personal business with the Lord Jesus

Christ and the claim He has upon each of our lives. Billy, you're going to die, and so am I and everyone else."

Billy prayed that day and received our Lord Jesus Christ. A week later, his mother, Dorothy, asked me to share at his funeral. Though heartbroken, with our Lord doing what only He can do, I was able to share a personal message of comfort and hope.

Six months later, I received a call from Billy's Aunt Cindy. I could tell that she was trying her best to hold back the tears.

"Bob, we're at Stringfellow Hospital with my daddy. He's in the advanced stage of cancer. The doctor just told us that he has only a few days to live. He wants to speak with you. Can you come now? We're in room 508."

"Sure, Cindy. I'll be right there."

The room was filled with family and loved ones overflowing into the hallway. Some were sobbing. Some, shocked with blank stares. The mood was quiet, somber, and very sad.

Cindy greeted me with a gentle hug, took my hand, and led me over to her daddy's bedside. Joyce, his devoted wife of 46 years, was there by his side, tightly holding his hand. His head was slightly elevated. He was very alert, sharp, and clear-minded; obviously, he'd been given no mind-altering medication.

Paul offered his hand to greet me as everyone else left the room. He and I were there together, alone. His handshake was firm, calm, and prolonged.

"Bob, thank you for coming. I met you briefly when our grandson, Billy, passed. We really haven't had an opportunity to get to know each other, but, if you're available, I would appreciate it so much, if you'd say a few words at my funeral service, and it looks like that's going to be pretty soon."

## One on One

I realized, right away that this was not a visit for me to comfort, console, or minister to someone else. This man was so calm and at peace, fearless, and radiating that unmistakable glow of the Holy Spirit. Our Heavenly Father brought me there that night to speak directly to me.

"Of course, Paul. I'd be honored to do that. Please share with me what's on your heart."

I slowly sat down in the straight back chair next to Paul's bed, slid it forward, and carefully prepared to listen.

*"Bob, after serving in World War Two, I returned home. Joyce and I eloped in 1950, and we began our family. I worked several years for the railroad before going to the pipe shop and then suddenly, 27 years ago, my heart exploded!*

*"They rushed me to the ER at The Piedmont Hospital. Doctors there told me to make peace with my Maker, because I would not be alive the next morning."*

He then paused, quietly reflecting, allowing me to go with him back to that decisive moment in his life. I dared not interrupt.

He continued: *"Bob, that's when I did one-on-one business with Jesus Christ. Over the years, I've been involved in several churches but never really felt comfortable or at home. I find no fault with anyone, and I tried, but organized religion has never been for me.*

*"Since that night, all those years ago in the ER, our Lord Jesus Christ has been more real to me than anyone else around. I deeply love Him, and I look forward to being set free and seeing Him face to face.*

*"At my funeral, please share whatever He puts on your heart, but the reason I'm led to ask you is because I trust that you will keep the attention on Jesus, not me!"*

"Paul, what do you mean when you say you did, 'one-on-one business with Jesus Christ?' Did you ask Him to heal you?"

## Learning to Love a Porcupine

*"Oh, no! I would never do that! I simply surrendered my will to His. My desire that night simply became to please only Him. If I lived or if I died, I wanted it to be in whatever way that would bring pleasure to my Lord. That's continued to be my desire for the last 27 years.*

*"Bob, I believe this time I am to die, and I have such a peace, even joy about it! Thank you for your willingness to share this time with me and my family."*

After a moment of silence, I took Paul's hand, thanked our Lord for his life, comfort for his family, and our visit. Then, I quietly made my way home.

The next day Paul was released from the hospital, moved to the modest, framed country house that he'd built for his family in 1957.

He'd been placed in the care of those precious souls from hospice, who were making him as comfortable as possible in his last hours.

It had been raining for several days, but that particular day, the sky was crystal-clear blue, the landscape, clean and beautiful. I went for a visit. Cindy greeted me at the door and quietly directed me to her daddy's bedside.

Paul was lying next to the bedroom window so he could see out between naps and feel the warmth of the sunshine.

His head again slightly elevated, oxygen tube in his nostrils, clear-plastic IV bag hanging on a stainless steel roller stand, saline with nourishment and meds steadily dripping down to and through the needle into the vein in his right hand, drop by drop, like a precision stopwatch, quietly, consistently, counting down a precious soul's final moments.

Paul slowly opened his eyes and looked at me. I was stunned! Even mesmerized! I have never looked into such sparkling and beautiful eyes, eyes as clear as the sky that day. It's like everything around us ceased to be! It's as if I was looking into the very eyes of Jesus Himself! I'm speechless!

## One on One

Though Paul was too weak to speak or lift his hand, his eyes said it all. I savored the moment and then quietly whispered, "You're doing one-on-one business with Jesus Christ, aren't you brother Paul?"

I noticed a twinkle of delight in his eyes and then a simple, gentle nod and smile. That was July 1996.

Through all the dangers, toils, snares, hardships, suffering, and mounting turbulence of this troubled world, with everything and everyone being threatened, is it possible to face reality and even death itself without being afraid?

In the intensifying storms of evil, terrorism, weapons of mass destruction, disease, natural disasters, and violent crime, can anyone be safe, secure, and anchored? Fearless?

The answer is absolutely YES! God uses our dear friend and brother in Christ, Paul Jenkins, to give us the key: **"One-on-one business with Jesus Christ!"**

Bro. Paul Jenkins

## Pity the Man

*If you've never seen*
*Your needs met out of nowhere,*
*If you've never known*
*The provision only He can give.*
*If you've never seen the Red Sea parted just for you,*
*My friend, you've never lived.*
*If you've never seen*
*The sparkle of life in a newborn's eyes*
*And seen that same sparkle*
*In the eyes of a saint*
*Telling this world goodbye.*
*If you've never known*
*The comfort only His Spirit can give,*
*My friend, you've never lived.*

*Pity the Man who trusts in his riches.*
*Pity the Man who trusts in his grain bins being full.*
*Pity the Man who's unaware of the other side.*
*Pity the Man who dreads to die.*

## CHAPTER 29

## *Trample on Love*

Dr. David Floyd is a successful, professional clergyman. He earned his Doctorate in Theology from his denomination's most respected seminary. He's had years of pastoral counseling and experience. Every church that called him as pastor grew rapidly, quickly becoming leaders in baptisms, membership, budget, building programs. Dr. Floyd was *"on top"* of his game!

He was highly esteemed, becoming known for his classic sermon from the Biblical text**, 2 Timothy 1:7,** entitled: *"God Has Not Given us a Spirit of Fear."* It went viral on the internet, and doors were opening for him, that is, until . . . his son, Robby rebelled and turned criminal.

Robby, 18, refused to submit to his dad and be a part of his religious fan club. He stubbornly refused to be a Dr. Floyd clone like he was expected to be. Instead, he rebelled and became a stray, homeless, crystal-methamphetamine addict.

Dr. Floyd was furious! He and his faithful Sunday school teacher wife, Patsy, Robby's mother, were embarrassed and publicly humiliated.

Robby's notorious reputation was destroying Dr. Floyd's career. The last thing he needed was a sinful, renegade son embarrassing him and his church!

Then, the final straw: Robby's behavior had gotten totally out of control! The chairman of the board of deacons called an emergency executive session to discuss "damage control" and possibly ask for Dr. Floyd's resignation.

Recognizing their responsibility to protect the church's reputation, the Deacon Board had to take action, of course, in as discreet a way as possible. Robby's behavior was bad for business.

Plus, the Bible says in **1 Timothy 3:5** that "if anyone does not know how to manage his own family, how can he take care of God's church?"

Dr. Floyd and Patsy had worked so hard to get where they were. Their career path had been flawless until this! Dr. Floyd was so tempted to blame himself.

Where did I go wrong? he often thought. *I've been so preoccupied with ministry that I neglected my own son! Trying so hard to succeed, I have miserably failed!*

In the midst of all the anger, fault finding, embarrassment, humiliation, and disappointment, Dr. Floyd and Patsy began to realize that there was something far more important to them than Dr. Floyd's profession and career. *It was their son!* Priorities were drastically shifting.

One evening, heartbroken, in the privacy of their home, they were praying and crying out to God, pleading with Him not to save Dr. Floyd's career—but to save their son! Suddenly there was a knock at the door.

"Who could that be this late?" they wondered.

He got up from his knees and went to the door. It was Joe, a boyhood friend of Robby.

"Come in, Joe. What can we do for you?"

"Dr. Floyd, sorry to bother you this late but, it's Robby. He's out of control. If something's not done, he'll kill himself, and I don't want to go to his funeral knowing I didn't try to help, but I don't know what to do!"

Dr. Floyd, in his younger years, had been trained Special Forces, US Army. Combat instinct took over.

"Joe, I've got a friend who has a condo in the Tennessee Mountains. He told me I could use it anytime. Could you deliver Robby to me up there?"

"Sure, I'll tell him it's a drug deal and that there could be trouble. He'd love to get in on that."

Dr. Floyd, as was his custom, took charge, his bag packed, mission engaged. No turning back!

"Patsy, I'm going to do whatever it takes to save our son. I'll be gone as long as necessary. The hospital emergency room isn't far from the condo, so if there's a problem with his coming off the drugs, I'll know where to take him.

"I'm also going to take Randy with me. He's been right where Robby is and has been through detox. He can provide counsel from experience."

Randy was a young man living at OFA. He had been strung out on methamphetamine and every other drug that was available.

One evening, a year earlier, Randy had overdosed. His so-called friends panicked, drove to the local Hospital Emergency Room, slowed down just long enough to open the door and push his lifeless body out onto the sidewalk, and then raced away.

Miraculously, Randy was rescued and lived. It took three weeks to stabilize his vital signs. After being released, he had nowhere to go. His mother wanted to take him in, but his stepdad wouldn't allow it.

Growing up, Randy had experienced the wrath of numerous angry stepdads. His mentally ill, guilt-ridden, troubled mom subconsciously felt like she deserved to be punished, and, therefore, was attracted to violent men who would beat her and her child!

Randy, living at OFA, had been clean for almost a year. It was obvious why Dr. Floyd wanted him to come along and be his medical advisor.

It was a five-hour drive to the point of confrontation. As soon as Robby saw his dad, he went into a rage!

The demons manifested! Hatred pouring out of him like a sewer! *Fast forward...3 a.m.*, Robby, arms folded, stubbornly planted in cab of truck, refusing to get out. It was unseasonably cold.

Dr. Floyd brought Robbie a blanket. Thanks, Daddy." The first kind words spoken to his dad in years.

"I know why you're doing this," he said.

"Why?" Floyd replied.

"FEAR!" he said in disgust.

Dr. Floyd, respected theologian, Bible scholar, and expert on overcoming fear, was introduced to himself that morning, and it took only one word from his wayward son: "FEAR!"

When the prophet Nathan showed up with God's mirror that fateful day, (**2 Samuel 12**), King David was introduced to the wretched, egotistical, full-of-pride, self-centered, despot he had become. Being respected, put on a pedestal, admired, and revered can cause one to take himself way too seriously. The drug addict Robby held up Nathan's mirror to his dad with one word! *FEAR!*

Had King David justified himself made excuses, or shifted the blame, his end would have been no less tragic than the other evil kings who had ruled Israel.

King David proved to be a man after God's own heart when his cry became **Psalm 51:4**: "Against you, you only, have I sinned and done what is evil in your sight, so that you are proved right when you speak and justified when you judge. **10** Create in me a pure heart, O God, and renew a steadfast spirit within me. **11** Do not cast me from your presence or take your Holy Spirit from me. **12** Restore to me the joy of your salvation and grant me a willing spirit, to sustain me. **13** Then I will teach transgressors your ways, and sinners will turn back to you."

Dr. David Floyd was also a man after God's own heart. He was broken, no longer a "know it all."

He woke up his accomplices, Robby's true friends, who cared more about him than avoiding his anger and wrath toward them.

There in the cold, standing by the truck window, Dr. Floyd confessed his sin.

"Jesus did not come to take us captive against our will. I have sinned. Robby, I'm sorry. Before they take you back, I want to ask you to please do just one thing."

"What?" he replied abruptly.

"Forgive me. Because if you don't forgive me, then you won't let me help you when you're ready."

"Okay! Get me out of here!" He said to his friends.

Dr. Floyd and Tommy headed home. Dr. Floyd broke the silence, "Randy, I blew it!"

"Dr. Floyd, it's going to be all right. I wish I had a dad who loved me enough to blow it!"

Some months later, after living the life of a stray vagabond, a couple of stints in jail, and compounded misery, Robby came home. He and his dad reconciled and have had a blessed relationship for many years.

Robby has no criminal record. He has been clean and living a responsible life for more than a decade. He's not the same person. Neither is Dr. Floyd.

Dr. David Floyd's ministry continues to "be fruitful and multiply" but in a more non-traditional, behind-the-scenes way.

Because of, *not in spite of,* their family's trial, he and Patsy are now qualified, by experience, to share hope with other families who are going through the same nightmare.

Dr. Floyd spends a lot more time serving behind the scenes these days. The residents at OFA know him as a personal friend, and he's not referred to as "doctor" but simply, "Brother David." He prefers that.

## Trampled on Love

*His momma and his daddy loved each other*
*and they loved their child.*
*He grew up in a home of provision and care,*
*then he went off wild.*
*Shook his fist in the face of God.*
*The pusher he wouldn't shove.*
*Sold his soul for holes in his arm.*
*He Trampled on Love.*

*He Trampled on Love, He Trampled on Love.*
*He spit in the face of mercy and grace.*
*He Trampled on Love.*
*The family's torn apart.*
*Heaven has a broken heart.*
*Where can the healing start?*
*He Trampled on Love.*

## Trample on Love

*It's so easy to point a finger of shame at the prodigal son*
*And arrogantly accuse him of being the only one.*
*But every time we worry or fear,*
*Every time we fail to forgive,*
*We must first reject the Father and the love He freely gives.*
*Unbelief calls God a liar and slanders his throne above.*
*Unbelief is just another way WE trample on love!*

*It won't be long until his fair-weather friends are gone.*
*It won't be long until he's left all alone.*
*It won't be long until he longs for home*
*And there he will find a love that says,*
*"Never mind that you trampled on love!*

*No more Trampling on Love. No more Trampling on Love.*
*No more spitting in the face of mercy and grace.*
*No more Trampling on Love.*
*The family's no longer apart.*
*Heaven has a grateful heart.*
*Forgiveness is where the healing starts.*
*No more Trampling on Love!"*

## CHAPTER 30

## Our Father's Arms International

How did a simple homebody, nobody, Alabama country boy, with no clue about other cultures, find himself on a hot, dry summer afternoon, drinking hot tea out of a filthy cup, in a broken-down, dilapidated bus in a forest outside of Southampton, England?

There with my guitar, playing, singing, and sharing my heart with a captive audience of unsanitary social rejects, pot-head hippies who were passing through, terrorizing neighborhoods; some were arrested, torn away from their children, and taken to jail. And there I was! Caught right in the middle of multiple dramas I had nothing to do with! So far from home and way too strange for real life! Must have been a dream, but it wasn't.

A few days later, naïve, slightly embarrassed, dumbfounded, with guitar, I shared my country love songs with the distinguished highbrow congregation in the beautiful, historic Westminster Chapel in London. The legendary Billy Graham had been there the week before. How do you follow that?

British Broadcasting Company doing a news special on the Christian Presence at Glastonbury Rock Festival 1993. Here they filmed Vic baptizing gypsy traveler. Bob far left with guitar.

Bob on gypsy traveler's bus

The world-renowned, highly respected, Greek and Hebrew scholar Westminster pastor, at the recommendation of an associate, reluctantly allowed me to share two songs he carefully censored and left me with these parting, kind words: "No one like you has ever, ever, sung here before! Goodbye!"

## Our Father's Arms International

Now, how did all that happen? How did an unlikely country boy like me wind up in these very strange places? Was I dreaming? Nope! It really happened!

Westminster Chapel Sanctuary

And that was just the beginning! Over these years, I've taken my guitar and shared in dangerous prisons, streets, jails, slums, and all kinds of unpleasant, heartbreaking, dark places, but, in stark contrast, I've also played concert tours in plush European theaters, all-age school classrooms, and even the famous Glastonbury, England, Rock Festival four consecutive years. There's no way to make this stuff up!

On one occasion, I was locked up for a day in a filthy, stuffy, old, overcrowded, run-down cell in Cape Town South Africa's Pollsmore Prison. I was there sharing my heart and songs with a violent group of gang inmates, most accused of capital murder and who had been there for years with a bad attitude waiting for trial. A white boy with a southern drawl and twelve-string guitar was unusual and amusing to them therefore, I had their attention as I shared my songs of God's unfailing love demonstrated through a violent, blood-soaked cross.

I kept thinking, Who am I, and how in hell did I wind up in this awful, heartbreaking place?

Later, on that same tour, I shared in the impoverished Township of Langa, where precious, malnourished souls were living under bridges and lean-to scrap-lumber and cardboard boxes! Open, raw sewage! Nights filled with screams of violence, rape, and rage! Orphan kids with nowhere to go, seemingly no hope!

Home seemed so far away! I knew that I would personally never be the same, but I also knew, as heartbreaking and uncomfortable as it was, I was destined to be there. So, I kept loving, hugging, listening, weeping, singing, and sharing the joy and hope that can come from only the Truth of the Gospel!

There were so many other prisons, orphanages, streets, concert tours, not only in South Africa but throughout UK and Ukraine.

One year I shared daily in a week of solo concerts in inner-city Istanbul, Turkey. 98% Muslim. Some radical. For an Alabama country boy like me, another very unlikely venue that I embraced and survived!

Over these years, I've been learning to live out of my comfort zone, and I'm so grateful to have discovered and now realize that *out of the comfort zone is where the miracles happen!*

The door to my non-conforming, wild ride opened in 1984, when an Englishman named Vic passed thru the small rural Northeast Alabama community of Williams, where we live.

After hearing Vic preach and his hearing the "Bug Zapper Tape" mentioned earlier, he and I began to connect as close friends with a mutual love for our Lord Jesus Christ and like passion to share His love off the beaten path.

We are *"peas out of the same pod."* Vic became and remains my mentor and dear friend. I jumped in his back pocket, so to speak, and it's been one glorious and exciting ride full of surprises ever since! He is truly a rare, unique, and amazing individual!

# Our Father's Arms International

**Introducing Vic Jacksopson,**
**Our Father's Arms International Director:**

The isolation, loneliness, fear, and deep, personal rejection of being abandoned is a hell that only an orphan could know. Most of us have grown up with a family and a place to call home. Try to imagine never having known that!

A state-supported institution may keep one alive physically, but a child needs much more than that to survive. Look in his eyes. It's the same terrified look you see in the eyes of a stray puppy that's just been run down, caught in a net, and thrown into an insect-infected cage.

His name is Vic. Being small in stature made the isolation that much more terrifying. It's no wonder his teenage years were ravaged by alcohol, fighting, and crime. That's what gangs do, and, when no one else wants you, the gang life is the only option, the only way to survive. That road, however, always leads to either prison or cemetery.

For Vic it was prison. Only 18 years old, locked in a solitary-confinement cell in the Winchester, England, Prison, Vic realized that no matter how clever or street smart he had become, he wasn't about to talk his way out of this one!

A rigid, worn-out bunk, filthy, no sheets, smelly blanket rolled up for a pillow was waiting for him. No toilet. Only a metal bucket slopped out twice a day! Dirty, stained, concrete floor, surrounded by brick walls; a huge, creepy, crawling cockroach was his only companion, hour after hour, while he sat there miserable, bored to tears.

Vic happened to notice the Gideon Bible when the guards took the handcuffs off and violently shoved him into the cell. He had no interest in the Bible, especially the 1611 King James Version that kept staring at him! He'd always thought that Christianity was for good people, and Vic knew he wasn't one, therefore, it was not for him!

**Vic, the gang member and thief**

He also wasn't a very good reader. His dyslexia had convinced him and others that he was "slow." But what does one do when there's no more bricks left to count? He picks up the Bible and slowly begins to try to comprehend.

Days later: "Who is this Jesus?" Vic thought. "Hey, He ain't what I thought He was! This is my kind of guy! He's tellin' those religious phonies just like it is . . . ..right in their face, 'You're a brood of vipers! Whitewashed tombs! Blind leadin' the blind!' Man, He made 'um mad enough to kill Him! Look how those religious big shots treated Him! And He didn't back down one bit!"

Then, at once, Vic realized, "But He had such mercy and love for no-good nobodies like me! That thief there on the cross . . . that's what I am, a thief! I wonder, did he ever know his mommy and dad? He was probably an orphan boy, too! Hey, he is me! Man! That thief asked Jesus to remember him and . . ."

The bunk in that cell became an altar. Alone, awkward, and even a bit confused, Vic knelt and prayed this sinner's prayer: "God, I'll give you 10 days to change my life. If you haven't done it by then, you've 'copped it!'" That's the Brits' way of saying, "Blown it!"

That was 10 September 1959. For more than half a century now, a countless number of souls would come to know this "my kind of guy Jesus" through the ministry of Vic Jackopson!

In 2010, Vic received another hand-delivered summons from the authorities. Only this time it was not an arrest warrant.

He was summoned to Windsor Castle, where he appeared before Queen Elizabeth as she personally distinguished and bestowed upon him one of the highest honors of his fellow countrymen.

Recognized for his years of selfless service in rescuing homeless children in Ukraine, her Majesty, the Queen presented Vic with the official honor of: MBE, "Member of the British Empire."

Vic has not only been rescuing orphans from the sewers and streets in Ukraine but has also been very active working with prison inmates and their families, homeless kids, and orphans in other parts of the world as well.

**Queen Elizabeth honoring Vic**

During the course of his ministry, Vic has been used by our Lord to birth, nurture, equip, and release dozens of other Christian ministries that continue to bring the living Gospel (*not just tracts and words but practical help*) to thousands of needy souls from Vietnam to South Africa, throughout Europe, US, daily expanding around the globe with the life of the Resurrected One Who is alive and Who reigns!

A tree is known by its fruit. Wisdom is vindicated by her children. Looking at the life and influence of this elderly statesman and confirmed man of God, even the most cynical skeptic would have to admit: "*God certainly did not 'cop it'!*"

Our Father's Arms, Jacksonville, Alabama, USA, under Vic's guidance, has been taken to another level of expanded service and influence. Since 1996, we have consciously set our hearts on learning to walk out and live the **1 Corinthians 13:8** "love of God that never fails and we are fruitful and multiplying throughout planet earth."

In the midst of all the heartbreak, misunderstandings, betrayals, and being victims of crimes many times, we are seeing hard-core drug addicts delivered, habitual criminals transformed, families restored, and the hopeless finding hope.

Quite simply, we are seeing Jesus do what He came here to do: "Seek and save those who are lost!" (**Luke 19:10**)

I've been honored to know and walk with Vic Jackopson since 1984. He and I have traveled through three continents together sharing God's love in the worst of prisons, streets, orphanages, schools, slums, even amidst those roving gypsy travelers.

I'm deeply humbled, honored, and appreciative of our Lord allowing me to walk with this man, whose life and service will be honored, cherished, and remembered long after he physically departs.

**Vic with orphans**

**Sue and Vic**

Sue, Vic's precious wife, was his closest companion and behind-the-scenes ministry partner for more than 40 years. She was liberated from her frail physical body in 2017. This was written for Vic and Sue:

## Little Flowers

We surely know if a flower's going to grow,
It's got to have the sun
Or it'll wilt one day and die away
Before its young life's begun,
Before its song is sung.
Heaven help the flowers that have no sun.

Listen as they play their magic song.
They lead the children, and they bring love to them
And they all sing along.
Like little flowers reaching for the Son.
They're little flowers,
Vic and Sue reflect the Son.

Sue found what true life's got
But she never was yours or mine.
She belongs to the only One Who
Can make life's words rhyme,
So, we don't mind, because,
Love forever keeps on working all the time!

Listen as they play their magic song.
They lead the children, and they bring love to them
And they all sing along.
Like little flowers reaching for the Son.
They're little flowers,
Vic and Sue reflect the Son.

## CHAPTER 31

## Dugger Mountain Music Hall

Call it "luck," a rare "twist of fate," or claim "the stars were lined up just right." No matter what it's called or whatever the claim, no one can deny that we are right in the middle of a bona fide miracle!

We know, without reservation or hesitation, it is the power, vision, provision, guidance, and demonstrated love of our Lord Jesus Christ!

Those who are reaching out to "the least of them" with no ambition but to please the Lord, are literally touching the heart of Almighty God! He confirms that He is pleased with unmistakable signs and wonders, and Dugger Mountain Music Hall is undeniably a sign and a wonder!

We have never had a fundraiser, foundation, or government grant. Our financial policy remains, "freely receive/freely give," and through the unsolicited support of people who care, we continue to be fruitful and multiply.

## Learning to Love a Porcupine

The High Profile of a Low Profile Ministry

The reason OFA keeps a low profile is to protect the dignity and privacy of our residents. Though many have experienced rehabilitation and have found effective transition into healthy community, OFA is not a rehab or a halfway house. We are, very simply, a Christ-centered family learning to love and care for each other.

## *The Dugger Mountain Music Hall Story*

### 2006

Chris, a dear friend who had owned and operated a recording studio for twenty or so years, decided to close the business and sell the building and equipment. He called one mid-morning.

"Bob, I have the recording equipment in climate-controlled storage and was planning to sell it on Ebay, but, in my prayer time this morning, I sensed our Father instructing me to donate it to Our Father's Arms."

"What would we do with it, Chris?" I asked, very puzzled.

"I have no idea." He said, "Our Lord said for me to donate it. Do with it as He wills. It now belongs to OFA, no strings attached."

With truck and trailer, we loaded up and hauled the state-of-the-art recording equipment to our men's home and stored it in one of the bedrooms. It was worth thousands of dollars!

We seldom know in advance how we will pay month-to-month bills, but our Lord always provides. Oftentimes, it's out of places we thought were nowhere, and, sometimes, it's just in time!

We were seriously considering selling the equipment. Perhaps this is the Lord's way of providing for continued operation, I thought.

I never had time to do more than consider selling it. A year went by.

## 2007

I received a surprise call from the Director of Missions of the Calhoun County Baptist Association.

"Bob, the Association has been deeded an abandoned church building out on Highway Nine about five miles south of Piedmont. The locals out there have made it clear that they don't need or want another church in their community! Could 'Our Father's Arms' use the building? We need to do something with it."

"I'm not sure," I replied. "We'll seek the Lord and get back with you."

As time would permit, I'd go to the church alone and simply walk around, sit, and prayerfully, quietly listen.

A week or so later, after countless hours of walking, sitting, praying, and listening, I called the Director and told him that we had a peace about it.

"Yes, let's go ahead with the paperwork. We look forward to seeing what the Lord has planned for us to do with it."

Drug addiction not only destroys brain cells and organs but also does terrible emotional and psychological damage to one's sense of self-worth, dignity, and self-respect. One of the therapeutic means of recovery is to "work with your hands."

We call it "Work Therapy." That old, abandoned church building became a perfect place for that to happen.

It just so happened, at that very appropriate time, our residents at "Reality Road" just happened to have the necessary skills to tear out walls, frame, put up and finish sheet rock, paint, run wire, lay flooring, repair plumbing, etc. Materials were provided just when needed, and within a couple of months, the sanctuary in that old church had been transformed into a "state-of-the-art" recording studio!

Nic, engineer in DMMH Control room.

Amazing! One has to see it to believe it! The equipment donated a year earlier got moved to its home, and the guys on "Reality Road" got their bedroom back!

## The "Come as You Are" Church

The Our Father's Arms family had been meeting for worship and Bible Study at 2:30 on Sunday afternoons since 1996. Our meetings are informal, seemingly unstructured, and more comfortable for the growing number of people who have been hurt by the strife, dissension, and division in some of our traditional churches.

The meetings usually last not more than one hour, but the informal fellowship, ministry in disguise, sometimes goes on into the night.

As soon as we took possession and got the power turned on, even in the midst of construction, we started having our Sunday-afternoon meetings there. The sign out front stirred some controversy.

**Controversial sign out front**

It attracted a number of "outcasts," but it also "spooked" some of the more respectable neighbors. After a year, one of the neighbors approached me and asked me to change it.

"Why?" I asked. "Didn't our Lord say it's the sick who need a physician?"

He replied, "Well, I guess you've got a good point," and then left.

Another neighbor sent word, asking if we needed to put up a 10-foot-high chain-link fence around the property with barbed wire across the top!

I then realized, it was not only time to change the sign but also to somehow reach out to our neighbors and let them know that, contrary to rumors, we weren't bringing dangerous criminals into the community.

## Learning to Love a Porcupine

That's just when my cousin Lloyd, the dobro player, happened to call.

"Bob, I'm in a Bluegrass band, and we love to play, but we need a place that's more family friendly, where our kids and their friends can come. What do you think about our playing out there at yall's church on some Saturday nights?" he asked.

"Bingo! Yes, Lloyd, let's do it! The timing is perfect! We'll have the ladies from OFA ladies' home, Eagle's Nest, prepare some food, and we'll open the doors for the neighbors. No charge! Since we're right across the road from the picturesque, Federal Reserve, "Dugger Mountain Wilderness" we can call it the "Dugger Mountain Music Hall Family Gatherin'!"

We were excited! The show was on! The sign was changed. We found our identity! The food, the fellowship, and the music was fun for the whole family. The bands came with no expectation of getting paid. We put an old, worn, cowboy boot on the corner of the stage for donations, and there was typically more than enough to cover everyone's expenses.

Tim Thompson is an international finger-pickin' guitar champion living in Nashville. His son Myles, then-16-year-old prodigy, played fiddle and violin with him. They are two of the most gifted musicians and songwriters anywhere. We became friends in 2010 as we traveled together in the UK doing a concert tour to raise the awareness of the plight of orphans in the Ukraine.

I invited them down to play for one of the DMMH shows. Everyone was awestruck! Theirs is a show that could cost high dollar for tickets to somewhere like Madison Square Garden in New York City, and here they were five miles south of Piedmont, Alabama, on Highway Nine at the "Dugger Mountain Music Hall"!

The night Tim and Myles played, Alan Rhodes, a TV producer from Huntsville, Alabama, just happened to stop by.

## Dugger Mountain Music Hall

Like everyone else, he was amazed. "Bob, this needs to be televised! I'm partners with a low-power TV station in North Alabama. As soon as you can get me a DVD, we'll start airing it at no cost," he said.

Our friend, Tom Potts of Potts Marketing and producer, Jamie Smith brought in the cameras and produced the first,"Dugger Mountain Music Hall" 30-minute TV program. Just a few weeks after it was aired in Huntsville, The Walk Christian Family Network picked it up, and we went from an audience of 40 once a month to a potential audience of more than 40,000,000 every week, with no cost to the ministry!

All that's been accomplished to date has been staffed by precious people who love the Lord and this ministry volunteering their time. We call it "Love Equity," and there continues to be a lot of it!

**DMMH Fellowship Hall**

In addition to The Walk Network, Dugger Mountain Music Hall is now being carried once a week on the Heartland Network (Formerly TNN), Alabama Public Television and Irish TV Network, with a potential of 150 million households and public schools.

The growth and popularity of the program attracted sponsors, which provided the necessary funds for OFA to build and operate an urgent-care free clinic near town. We also periodically receive anonymous gifts in the mail from other parts of the country.

## Come One, Come All

When the road gets rough,
People tend to get uptight.
Seems that instead of love
Too many want to fuss and fight,
Whine, complain and shift the blame,
Double the trouble and add to the struggle
Of an already difficult time.
For our own sake, why don't we take a break
And head out to Highway Nine
Where the music's fine,
Find a place to unwind,
Have a good time
With some gooood friends of mine!
Come One, Come All to the

Dugger Mountain Music Hall!

## CHAPTER 32

# Falling in Love With God's Word

In their home, you will find the family Bible sitting in the middle of the coffee table. It's been there ever since we can remember. It sits there like a vase of artificial flowers, gathering dust. The thick, faded, blue, imitation-leather front cover carries that familiar painting of Jesus, the little boy in a robe, confidently standing there in the temple instructing the amazed scribes and elders. The pages look like they're probably stuck together.

It's a much more sacred ornament than a vase of flowers, though. You dare not place anything on top of it, and you dare not move it, or God's wrath will zap you, and He'll use an angry mother hen the grandkids call "Maw-Maw" to do it! Oh, how she loves the Lord, or so we've always been told.

Maw-Maw and Big Daddy are at church every time the doors open. We celebrated their 60th wedding anniversary in the fellowship hall last Sunday evening.

**Living room decorations**

No one will admit it, but we were all pretending. Though they live in the same house, she's been shunning and pouting with him for the past 50 years! She caught him being unfaithful to her, and she's not about to forgive or forget. They live in opposite ends of the same house with an impenetrable wall of silence between them.

Is the book we call the Holy Bible merely an ornament or maybe an amulet like *a rabbit's foot* kept close by for good luck, or is it really the Word of Almighty God?

After all, like any other book, it was written by mortal men, and no one seems to understand it anyway, except maybe our professional preachers, and so many of them have different interpretations and opinions.

It can be very confusing for us common folks. We humans have always had a tendency to be superstitious. Some believe that's the only thing the Holy Bible is good for.

I saw in the newspaper recently that a local university was hosting a public debate between a Muslim scholar from the East and a Christian scholar from the West.

## Falling in Love With God's Word

Which is the authentic word of God, the Quran or what we call the Holy Bible? It appears that one's opinion will depend on which part of the world he's born, raised, and educated in. Me, I'm born and bred Bible Belt!

At first, the newspaper article offended me. I was disgusted and defensive even at the suggestion that the ornament of our sacred tradition might be challenged!

Why was I offended? Was it because I'm insecure and, therefore, feel threatened? Was it because I'm really not convinced that what I've always been taught and professed to believe is really true?

The Bible Belt in America is highly populated with people who profess to be Christians, go to church, quote Scripture, but in reality, when you get right down to it, many of them tend to be anything but loving, kind, and pleasant to be around!

But, as we keep an open mind and try not be too judgmental of the judgmental ones, we'll begin to notice in our midst a few precious souls who are obviously discovering within the Holy Bible a supernatural power to live, forgive, be set free, and enjoy the abundant life Jesus refers to in *John 10:10* regardless of external circumstances.

Those few precious souls have a deep inner peace even when they're going through what others perceive to be tragedy. They don't debate. They simply and calmly demonstrate.

**John 5:39:** "You search the Scriptures daily for in them you think you have life but it's they which testify of me."

We are discovering from personal and shared experience that the Holy Bible is indeed the infallible, inspired Word of Almighty God but, just as Isaiah expressed thousands of years ago: it's not revealed to those "who honor Him with their lips and yet their hearts are far from Him." **Isaiah Chapter 29:11–13**

When the Holy Bible is approached in a spirit of humility, reverence, respect, and openness, then the written document comes alive, *revelation is imparted,* and another life begins to be transformed! Blind spiritual eyes are opened!

*"Amazing Grace how sweet the sound, that saved a wretch like me. I once was lost but now I'm found, was blind but now I see"* becomes very personal and very real!

If we miss the love commandment, we miss it all! So simple that a child can see it, while an expert theologian will oftentimes overlook it! The Living Word says through the written Word, "I love you with a love that never fails; with a love that is greater than your selfishness and sin."

## He Gives His Word

*Lost and so confused,*
*A stranger in a foreign land*
*Living in desperation*
*I life I could not understand.*
*Afraid to place my faith in someone*
*That I could not see*
*Until I heard a still, small voice calling out for me.*

*He Gives His Word*
*To shine and show the way.*
*He Gives His Word*
*We will see Him face to face.*
*It's just got to be the sweetest sound I've ever heard.*
*He Gives His Word.*

## Falling in Love With God's Word

*Oh yes, there's still trouble.*
*I still get weary from the load.*
*I stumble and I struggle sometimes*
*Down life's rough and rocky road.*
*And when all seems dark about me, I look up and I can see*
*The bright and Morning Star forever,*
*Shining out for me.*
*He Gives His Word.*

# CHAPTER 33

## Making Disciples One Day at a Time

The word "disciple" comes from the word "discipline." Most of those who come to live with us at OFA have no clue as to what it means to have any discipline in their lives. They've been allowed to run wild, with no family covering or guidance.

So, how can someone personally be led to the delightful, joyful fountain of Living Water we find in the Bible, without first being introduced to effective study habits and discipline?

We are discovering a way that's effective for some: The OFA Proverb for the Day.

There are so many precious souls around us who can't read. Many hide it well but are too embarrassed to admit it. My precious wife, Patti, a retired elementary school teacher, researched, collected materials, and began teaching her first OFA student to read, but he ran away to his old, addiction lifestyle before there could be any progress.

We look forward one day to being able to address this need more effectively, but, for now, we simply let our residents know that if you can't read, simply trust someone to read it for you, or each day anyone can use their phone and go to Our-Fathers-Arms.net and listen; also, on Mondays, we come together from 6 to 7 as a group for The OFA Proverbs for the Day Bible Study that is streamed and posted on Facebook, so anyone can watch and listen on their phone at any time.

A Bible that has come alive

The book of Proverbs has 31 chapters, one for each day of the month. As we read the Proverb for each Day, inspired by the Holy Spirit, we discover a springboard and commentary to the rest of Scripture.

Proverbs, the doorway of wisdom, provides an excellent and effective entrance into the wonders and transforming power of the *Living Word* found within the pages of the *written Word*!

Over the years, we have discovered seven keys that repeatedly help unlock the deeper meaning, bringing application to everyday life and making the text applicable, relevant, and sacred:

## Making Disciples One Day at a Time

# Key 1

*The Mysterious, Almighty, Creator God's heart toward each of us is affection, not rejection.*

The wrath of God we read about in the Old Testament is the consequence of man's rebellion against the Almighty's pre-ordained Law.

If someone without a parachute defiantly jumps out of an airplane in flight, the law of gravity is fulfilled, impersonally, without any regard or consideration of the consequence!

God is not vicious and mean because He won't reverse His law to accommodate our rebellion! The same applies to His spiritual laws. The wrath of God is consequence, not vengeance!

The longer we live, the more suffering we see and experience. This can cause one to draw the conclusion that God is unloving and uncaring, even a bully and serial killer of the innocent!

Some had rather conclude that He doesn't even exist! This is the false foundation of atheism! That's what drove me deeper into addiction.

If one is willing to let go of his or her prideful opinions and simply look and consider the Cross, perception and attitude will radically be transformed!

We can never question the love of God when considering the Cross of the Lord Jesus Christ and what was taking place at that moment in history! He *reaped* what you and I have sown and will sow! The law of the Spirit of Life in Christ Jesus supersedes the Law of sin and death! **Romans 8:2**

Paul, the Apostle and writer of most of the New Testament, put it this way: ***1 Corinthians 2:2:*** "For I determined not to know anything among you except Jesus Christ and Him crucified."

## Key 2

### *You don't need a "holy go-between."*

Solomon, the writer of Proverbs, violated the wisdom he was used to imparting and, thus, he died a fool. The Bible documents this so that we will not exalt any man. **1 Kings 11:4–11**

Do not put anyone on a pedestal, even the man or woman God chooses to speak through. The Holy Spirit is your Teacher, and the Word is for you personally. You have a personal invitation and direct access by the Blood of Jesus to approach the Perfect, Holy Almighty One!

Remember, the Creator has copyrighted your thumbprint! That means you are unique and very precious and special to Him as if you were His only child!

**Hebrews 4:6:** "Let us therefore come boldly to the throne of grace, that we may obtain mercy and find grace to help in our time of need."

**1 John 2:27:** "But the anointing (sacred appointment) which you have received from Him abides in you, and you do not need that anyone teach you; but as the same anointing teaches you concerning all things, and is true, and is not a lie, and just as it has taught you, you will abide in Him."

## Key 3

### *It's all about your ongoing thought life.*

Down through the endless pages of time, generation after generation, the Holy Bible has shown the unprecedented, amazing ability to transcend and communicate effectively with people from every culture and all walks of life. This is accomplished through the effective use of parables, symbolism, and allegories wrapped in the most creative, brilliant literary presentation ever penned. Even William Shakespeare acknowledged reverent admiration for the greatest literature ever given to man!

The Bible stories are inspired to give insight and revelation of one's thought life and God's unfailing, perfect, personal, forgiving love that lights the way to personal revival and freedom! The Bible also reveals how one can find the inner strength and power to live it out! Now, how amazing is that!!!

**Hebrews 4:12** "For the word of God is living and powerful, and sharper than any two-edged sword, piercing even to the division of soul and spirit, and of joints and marrow, and *is a discerner of the thoughts and intents of the heart.*"

**Psalm 119:105:** "Thy word is a lamp to my feet and a light to my path."

Your heart is your subconscious mind, the way you've been programmed to think as you make decisions and navigate your way through life. The thoughts you choose to entertain become the programming of your life's daily experience and the expression of your earthly life's journey.

Therefore, if any real personal progress is to be made, it will first happen "within," not "without."

Your heart is your garden. You and you alone are the garden keeper. The Spirit of our Lord Jesus offers to "come in" and intimately connect with you, to co-labor, teaching you to "bring every thought captive to the obedience of Him" **2 Corinthians 10:5** and also to assist you in meditating on "the things that are true, noble, just, pure, lovely, worthy of virtue and worthy of praise" **Philippians 4:8.**

**Proverbs 4:23** "Keep (watch over) your heart with all diligence, for out of it spring the issues of life."

## Key 4

*In the final analysis, all that really matters is, "Do you know the Man?"*

All of life's experiences, circumstances, trials, triumphs, events personal and global, serve the ultimate purpose of bringing human beings, created in His likeness, into an intimate, personal, forever-lasting, love relationship with our Creator. It's in this relationship one becomes like Him! **1 John 3:2**

## Key 5

*The way to knowing Him is found in trusting Him, not in analyzing and trying to understand Him.*

A finite mind is incapable of comprehending infinite reality, simply because the finite mind is confined to concepts derived through the five physical senses.

Therefore, if we're to truly enjoy the journey, we must accept that **Life is a miracle to be lived, not a mystery to be solved!**

The entire Bible is for the purpose of communicating what is revealed in these two verses:

**Proverbs 3:5,6** "Trust in the LORD with all your heart, and lean not on your own understanding; In all your ways acknowledge (Hebrew word, *yadah* meaning "know") Him, and He shall direct your paths."

## Key 6

*"Correction is not rejection"*

Correction is simply love showing us a more excellent way to live.
**Proverbs 3:11, 12**

"My son, do not despise the chastening of the LORD, Nor detest His correction; For whom the LORD loves He corrects, Just as a father the son in whom he delights."

## *Key 7*

### *"We get nothing from God except that which we receive" 1 Corinthians 4:7*

"For who makes you differ from another? And what do you have that you did not receive? Now if you did indeed receive it, why do you boast as if you had not received it?" Oftentimes we quote this confession together before our group Bible studies:

> *"I don't do right to be right.*
> *I do right because I am right.*
> *I am right because He is making me right.*
> *He's making me right because I surrender*
> *In the arms of my Father and receive His Love.*
> *I get nothing from God except that which I receive*
> *and I'm ready to receive."*

Here's a few definitions we keep in mind as we study:

**WICKEDNESS**

Unbelief (nothing more wicked than calling God a liar)

**FOOL**

One who is not teachable and will not come to the Light. ***Proverbs 1:7***

**WISE MAN**
>One who is teachable and will come to the Light. ***Proverbs 2:3, 13:1***

**RIGHTEOUSNESS**
>Right "thinking" ***Proverbs 12:5***

**ADULTERY**
>Harlotry which is Idolatry ***Proverbs 29:3***
>Trying to find life in idols that are void of life (pacifiers)

**IDOLATRY**
>Trying to meet a legitimate need in an illegitimate way.
>A pacifier (idol) has no life, therefore can never satisfy.

**BREAD**
>Satisfier (The supply of every need) ***John 6:48***

**FEAR of GOD**
>Fear of missing Him. ***Proverbs 14:26, 27***

**THE LAW**
>"Love At Work"
>*"Lay your life down, no hook in it, forgiving love"* that fulfills the law.
>***Galatians 5:14, Romans 13:10***

**GOING SURETY**
>Co-dependency clinging. Taking responsibility for another.
>***Proverbs 6:1, Luke 14:26***

**HOUSE**
is you. *1 Peter 2:5, 1 Corinthians 3:9*

**WINE**
Often, but not always alcohol.
Wine is whatever leads one astray (idols which are pacifiers)
**Proverbs 20:1, 2 Corinthians 11:3, Proverbs 31:10–31, Genesis 1:2**

**LET**
"Living and Expressing Truth"
Implies the natural state for the *2 Corinthians 5:17* "new creature."

**PRIDE**
**P**itiful, **R**ebellious, "**I**" being **D**eceived and **E**xalted

**HUMBLE**
**H**aving **U**nderstanding of **M**y **B**roken, **L**owly **E**xistence

**HOPE**
**H**aving an **O**vercoming **P**erspective on **E**verything

**LOVE**
**L**osing **O**neself in the **V**ictor's **E**mbrace.

**FLESH**
**F**orsaking **L**ove, **E**mbracing **S**elfishness and **H**ell.

**SPIRIT**
**S**urrendered to the **P**owerful, **I**nvincible, **R**edeemer **I**nspired by **T**ruth

**FAITH**
Finding the Awesome Invisible Truth of Heaven

**FORGIVE**
Finding Opportunity to Release God's Invincible Virtue in the Earth.

**SHAME**
Satan's Hellish Attack on ME

**HATE**
Harboring Awful Toxic Energy

**LUST**
Living Under Sensual Torment

**EVIL**
Expressing the Void of Internal Loneliness

**DENIAL**
Don't Even Notice It's A Lie

**GUILT**
Going Under In Living Torment

# Caller ID

*Someone's constantly calling to talk with me in my head.*
*It may be a friend with the words of life*
*Or it may be a foe who's wanting me dead.*
*Thank God for His technology.*
*I can choose who I let talk to me.*
*It's called, "bringing thoughts captive"*
*To the truth that will set you free!*
*Thank God, thank God, thank God for Caller ID!*

*Caller ID,*
*God's way of protecting me.*
*Called ID, Caller ID.*
*I can answer the phone or I can leave it alone.*
*No more soul sellin', God rebellin', aggravatin', agitatin',*
*Messed-up, stressed-out, full-of-doubt pest a-pesterin' me!*
*Thank God, thank God, thank God for Caller ID!*
*Just like a prospector pannin' for gold,*
*I pocket the truth of God's Word,*
*Let the evil lies go.*
*Jesus lives in me, and He's saving my soul*
*As He sets me free!*
*He's helping me pay attention*
*To the Caller ID!*

## "The Final Analysis

Stretch out on this couch, open up your mind.
Dig back into your past, it's analyzing time.
You just might be a schizophrenic,
Masochistic and sadistic, too.
If they don't know what to call you,
Any ten-dollar word will do.

Don't try to avoid the wisdom of Sigmund Freud.
If you think your thinkin's on the blink,
You can sell out to a shrink.
After all, it's a crazy world,
Everybody's fighting to cope.
Help fill up the padded rooms,
Legalize a little more dope.

You can pickle your brain with booze, smoke your head with grass.
Or you can get you a case of religion, child
But none of that junk will last.
You can bury your head in the sand,
Bet your life on some retirement plan
But in The Final Analysis,
All that really matters is:
Do You Know the Man?

*You will reject Him or else you will receive Him.*
*You will deny Him or else you will believe Him.*
*And He says He's the Son of God*
*And He's offering you His Hand.*
*In the Final Analysis, all that really matters is:*
*Do you know the Man?*

# APPENDIX A

## *Pacifier or Satisfier*

The child is starving, emaciated, dehydrated, so much so that she has no more tears left to cry. Her fearful screams have diminished into soft sobs and whimpers, yet the horror and fear can still be seen in her little bulging eyes. Her body is a skeleton. There can be no greater heartbreak than witnessing this!

No matter how frantic I might be to save her, *I'm helpless! I'm paralyzed! Tormented*, as I'm forced to watch the precious little one's life ebb away . . .

 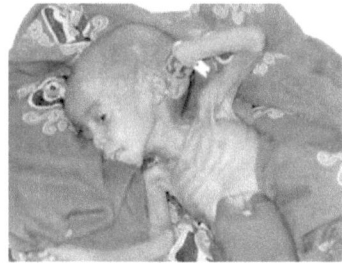 

**A Nightmare Dream**

## Learning to Love a Porcupine

All I'm able to do is cry out to God, but I doubt if that will make any difference. So many cry out to God, yet they still suffer and die!

There's so much "God is love" talk but so little "God is love" evidence! I choose to be a realist, and this child is starving to death! Every time I hear, "God loves you," I feel insulted!

What is that? I can't believe my eyes! Lying right next to the dying child is a baby bottle full of nourishing milk, but there's no one to feed her, and here I sit paralyzed!

Hopelessness! Curse God and die! If only I could die!

My tears, stress, fears, anger, and anguish are so consuming that I have no time to even consider the mysterious, faint, vague, elusive, almost indistinguishable silhouette of an angelic figure floating somewhere in the periphery. I'm way too angry and preoccupied with what I see as the problem that must be solved now!

If there is an Almighty, loving God, then why does He let this terrible injustice happen? Why doesn't He help me get up and help this child? I would do anything to save her, and I'm totally frustrated and angry because I can't!

The child is innocent and does not deserve this! I don't deserve this!

Finally, at last, she breathes her last. Her suffering is over. I start to notice a dried-out, brittle, torn, pacifier right next to her little mouth. Trying to save herself, she had been desperately and frantically sucking on that lifeless thing!

Her survival instinct engaged; she was intuitively consumed and obsessed with staying alive, trying to get her need met! Nothing else mattered.

Pacifiers are not satisfiers and never can be! All the child could do was suck on that lifeless, empty rubber nipple! I watched her die when

## Appendix A: Pacifier or Satisfier

all the nourishment she needed was lying right next to her! "Insult to injury" is an understatement!

My heart pounding, body shaking, in a cold sweat, I'm crying . . . as I awaken! What? A dream? Why?

The nightmare is over—or is it? I should be relieved, but I'm not. The anxiety and emotional turmoil won't go away! I'm confused and have many questions!

Here I am, years later, and the vivid duress of that dream still haunts me.

Who was that child? Why was I paralyzed and unable to help? What's the significance, if any, of the pacifier and the milk next to her? Why was I blaming God?

Oh, I nearly forgot, but, now I faintly recall, "Who was that vague, elusive, mysterious silhouette figure there in the shadows? The one I considered irrelevant.

## Lessons Being Learned

### Lesson 1: A dream is the subconscious mind being revealed.

The conscious mind is involved with the task of cyphering through the finite externals we perceive through our five senses, drawing conclusions, making judgments, establishing opinions, etc.

Then there's the subconscious mind, the part of us that never sleeps. The Bible refers to the subconscious mind as one's "heart," e.g., **Proverbs 4:23** NIV: "Above all else, guard your HEART, for everything you do flows from it."

The subconscious is our guidance system. It's programmed through the conscious mind, the counsel, opinions, and thoughts we choose to entertain.

### *Lesson 2: The starving child and the paralyzed witness represents all of humanity.*

Notice the way we feed our fears, shift blame, find fault, complain, stress out, helplessly overwhelmed with needs that are not being met, suffering, and death! We're frantically fighting to survive yet hopelessly dying like a desperate, deprived, starving child, and there's absolutely nothing we can do to stop it!

Sure, there's some happy, healthy people seemingly enjoying life on Earth, but many of them are living in denial. An escalating number are finding solace in medication. We have become masters in manipulating and controlling our brain chemistry, but it's only for those who can afford it, and it never lasts. What goes up will come down!

There are a few, however, who have found the key to peace of mind, regardless of external circumstances, the ones who have discovered how to partake of the life-sustaining, nutritious milk, those who are no longer interested in pacifiers. Is it possible for me to join them? If so, then how?

### *Lesson 3: The pacifiers are idols, other gods before the real Almighty, Sovereign, Creator God.*

Many, if not most of us, find ourselves desperately trying to meet our own needs by clinging and trying to possess that which is sterile and passing away, that which has no life. See **Psalm 135:15–18**. We keep trying to meet our legitimate need in illegitimate ways: pacifiers!

We are desperately trying to meet this need by selfishly grabbing and trying to protect our idols: pacifiers!

Obviously, a drug addict's drug is a pacifier but there's also socially acceptable, even encouraged and promoted pacifiers that are just as empty

## Appendix A: Pacifier or Satisfier

and deadly. It can be a career, even a ministry, a financial portfolio, shopping at the mall or online, the reputation of an institution, even a soccer, baseball, or football team!

Whatever is my primary preoccupation in life is my god! Often times the pacifier can be another person. This is the essence of codependency—trying to possess each other.

Religious dogma is definitely one. Oftentimes, we become culturally indoctrinated to worship an idea or concept of Jesus, and we call ourselves "Christians," or it may be a concept of Mohammed, and we call ourselves "Muslims," etc.

One of the ways we can recognize a pacifier is that we feel threatened and get offended if it's challenged. This is why there's so many religious wars! We're fighting over our pacifiers!

Anger and offense are the expressions of insecurity. Insecurity is the result of trusting a false security. A false security is an idol (pacifier).

### *Lesson 4: The gavel gets in the way and blinds us.*

In the dream I was judging God. **Romans 9:20.** I am the clay. He is the potter, and, in my self-willed arrogance, I was telling Him how it ought to be!

This blinded me to the elusive, mysterious Spirit who was waiting in the shadows to help. I selfishly had no time for the helper who was there and available.

The Helper is the Holy Spirit. The Holy Spirit, like a dove, is elusive, sensitive, peaceful, gentle and comes only when and where welcomed. My self-will and wanting to take matters into my own hands was my rejecting the only One Who was there to help! The silhouette, the One I gave little notice, was the Savior Himself!

### Lesson 5: I'm incapable of being another's Savior.

Only the Savior can save! The prayer of faith allows Him to invade the situation that I perceive to be a dilemma or problem. The prayer of fear is my taking my idol to God and pleading with Him to help! To pray effectively, I must have no other gods (personal pacifiers) before Him! See **Luke 14:26–33**.

### Lesson 6: God, Who is love, is not responsible for suffering and death.

Suffering and death are the direct result of our rebellion against Him! The innocent child is suffering the consequences of corporate sin and rebellion.

*Self-will is the illegitimate tyrant!* Yet, our Lord never shames or condemns (**John 3:17**) We cannot help being idolaters, until we see the Light of His personal Love.

### Lesson 7: Our deepest need is already met.

When one looks to the Cross, Who that Man was and is one can never, ever question His love and care! You are significant!

Your Creator copyrighted your thumbprint, gave you the ability to think and knows your thoughts before you even think them! He loves you as if you were His only child! In His eyes, you are perfect! You are worthy! His Blood has cleansed you. Please read **John 15:3**, rejoice, and enjoy the nourishing milk! Pacifiers are no longer needed, and now you are in a position for the Spirit of the Savior to use you in helping others.

The "how to" as presented in the sacred text known as the Holy Bible and the personal appropriation of every promise is: **1 John 4:19 NIV:** "We love Him because HE FIRST LOVED US."

# Appendix A: Pacifier or Satisfier

The Creator copyrighted
your thumb print

Be still. Let your soul be quiet. Consider His Cross. The awakening will come. The more aware we become of Him and His personal love, the less inclined we will be to have other gods before Him.

**Isaiah 45:22** "Look unto Me and be saved all ye ends of the earth. I am God and there is no other."

**John 15:12** "But I, when I am lifted up from the earth, will draw all men to myself."

"Jesus loves me—this I know." If it gets any more complicated than that, then we miss it!

As we personally awaken, the elusive Holy Spirit comes in to heal our paralysis so that He can feed the child, using non-judgmental, loving human beings to do it!

## Need Inside of Me

*I used to sit around and wonder,*
*What in the world am I doing here?*
*There's got to be more to life*
*Than living in a constant fear.*

## Learning to Love a Porcupine

*I even tried to hide,*
*So lonely inside.*
*Scared to death of dying down here,*
*Dying all alone down here.*

*Every time I'd pass the graveyard,*
*I'd turn and look the other way.*
*I couldn't bear to face the reality that me*
*And my loved ones would die one day.*
*Like an old, scared, and scroungy dog gone stray*
*Until Jesus took me in and began to love my fear away.*

*There is a need inside of you and me*
*Only He can satisfy.*
*When I think of all He's done for you and me,*
*Tears of joy begin to fill my eyes.*
*All was so hopeless 'til He saved me,*
*Cleansed by His precious blood*
*He set another captive free.*
*There is a need inside of you and me*
*Only Jesus can satisfy.*

# APPENDIX B

## The Window

*I* find myself crowded into the back corner of what appears to be the fuselage of a gigantic spacecraft. I begin hearing the sounds of turmoil, misery, and anguish.

Babies are screaming! Men, women and children are dying. The screams of people fighting each other is sucking the life out of me!

Hundreds of thousands, if not millions, are pulling, scratching, clawing, biting, walking on and over each other, shifting blame, finding fault, and fighting to survive.

**The window**

## Learning to Love a Porcupine

**Nowhere to escape**

It's terribly overcrowded in here! The heat, the noise is unbearable, and it never stops. There's nowhere to escape! The horrible stench of death is in this place.

There are a few pockets of quietness and superficial serenity, but even there, the people are on the verge of panic, pretending to have peace. They can't sit still and are obviously terrified of silence.

It's getting more difficult to breathe! I'm about to suffocate! Masses of people gasping for breath. Some are giving up! No hope! They are even killing themselves! It's so hostile and contaminated in here that people are actually stalking and killing each other!

More and more are even finding a temporary escape by being entertained by the violence! Some people are trying every imaginable type of drug, trying to escape their pain and misery! Many are drinking gallons and gallons of alcohol that is constantly flowing through their veins and brains, which serves only to amplify the confusion and insanity!

Where am I? Will I eventually wake up and realize this is a nightmare, not reality? I hope so, but I don't think so! What's going on? Why are we here? Is there any purpose in this insanity? How can I escape??

I then begin to notice the constant vibration, the rushing sound of wind, but I can't feel it. We must be in flight. The intensity of the wind must mean we are moving at a tremendous rate of speed.

## Appendix B: The Window

That's it! I'm trapped inside some sort of huge spacecraft with billions of terrified people who are also wondering how we got here and where are we going.

My eyes begin to glance above the dense, polluted sea of sick humanity toward what must be the front of the spacecraft. I notice there a large, vast platform leading up to a gigantic window of some sort. There are a few people climbing up to the platform and looking out the window. What do they see?

A brilliant, beautiful light begins to swirl around them. They begin to glow! They are being changed, transformed! They look for only a moment, turn and move back toward the crowd to help others to the platform so they, too, can gaze out the window and experience the Light

More and more people are climbing up, staring out that window, energized with hope and covered with light! Some are shouting and dancing!

What do they see that brings that glow to their smiling faces? Where is this spacecraft going? Do they see our destination? I can't see out that window from here, but I sure can see them! Something miraculous and dramatic is happening to those people!

I also notice that, once a person looks out that window and becomes "enlightened," that person must keep going back to look again and again, or else the darkness, misery, and sorrow of the crowd below will seduce them and cause the light to diminish. Eventually, they lose their hope. Looking out that window obviously recharges them. They must keep going back to look, again and again.

Amazing! Just as I was about to lose all hope, I noticed the light on those people.

I've got to get to that window! No matter what! I start shoving my way through the crowd. As I struggle to move forward, people start clinging to me, trying to keep me from going forward! I shake them off!

I must not get distracted! I've got to reach that window! I've got to see what those Light people see that gives them that glow, that joy, that hope! If I can just look out that window, then, perhaps, I can get the Light, too!

I've been kicked to the floor again! A terrible sharp pain in my back! I scream! I've lost all sense of direction! I can't see where to go!

As I lay there bleeding, about to give up, some dear soul comes out of nowhere, wipes my brow, and helps me to my feet again. I turn to thank her, and she's not there! Who was she? No time for that! I've got to keep moving! I'm getting closer now!

I hear people scream in anger: *"Stay away from that platform! Don't go to that window! You're crazy! Stay down here with us! The people on that platform are religious fanatics! They've gone off the deep end! We'll have nothing else to do with you if you go up there! It's not real! It's superstition, a myth! It's a cult! New Age! We have the answer! Stay down here with us! Be one of us! Bow down with us! Bow down to us!*

I then realize how desperate those people are to use me and to control me! But then again, maybe they're right. Maybe it is just a myth. After all, I don't want to waste my life chasing some fairy tale! I'd hate to be considered a religious fanatic who's gone off the deep end!

I've got to protect my reputation. I want people to respect me. I want my family to be proud of me. If I go toward that platform, they will think I'm weak. It will be embarrassing for me and for my family. They will probably disown me!

I'll just settle down right here, mind my own business, and do what I'm told. A day goes by, a week, a month, a year, then two, three. What's happening to time?

I'm miserable, empty, and haunted by loneliness and fear. Everything is so mundane, so meaningless. Is this all there is to life?

# Appendix B: The Window

The people in darkness invite me to play games with them. They say it's their way of *"coping with stress,"* which is just another way of saying, *"help ignore the misery, destruction, and death that is stalking each of us!"*

They offer me drinks to drink, pills to swallow, and smoke to inhale. They offer me extravagant entertainment to keep my mind off of the slaughter. They're trying to help me forget how frightened and miserable I am; and they may not admit it, but it's obvious, they are unhappy and miserable, too!

The drinks, pills, smoke, and entertainment do seem to work for a while but when the effect wears off, I'm more frightened and miserable than before! I need more drink, pills, smoke, and entertainment. It's an endless downward spiral into hell!

To complicate my misery, I'm haunted by those who left the crowd to climb to the platform and look out that window. I try to forget; but their radiance, joy, and hope won't leave me alone!

I'm getting old! Time is marching on, unhindered, steadfast cadence, and there's nothing any of us can do about it! We have no choice in the matter!

But I do have a personal choice about whether or not to move toward that platform and window! It will mean being rejected by people of darkness that I'll never be able to please anyway!

I can choose to stay here, take dope, play games, be like them, and die in the desperation, futility, and vanity of it all, or I can let go and go for it!

That's what I've decided to do! Though none go with me, I still will follow. No turning back! No turning back!

As I move toward the platform, the ridicule starts again! I can feel a magnetic pull from the people of darkness who surround me. It pressures me to pull back! I'm caught between two forces. The hope of the window is calling, while the people of darkness are trying to cling.

## Learning to Love a Porcupine

I submit to the higher call and resist the lower! One more step, then another! All energy depleted. I collapse!

I can go no further in my own strength. I look up and begin to see people of Light reaching toward me! I made it to the platform!!

The people of Light are so loving, caring, compassionate, encouraging! I'm receiving strength from them! I'm climbing up! I want more than anything to see what they see!

"Wait!" one of the people of Light says abruptly!

"You can't come up here with that mask on!"

"What mask?" I'm puzzled! I don't have on a mask!"

"It's the mask you've allowed the people of darkness to put on you.

"The platform is a place of reality and truth. The domain of darkness is a place of pretense and lies. You have on a mask that you've been trained to hide behind in order to get people of darkness to accept you. You've been taught to believe that your self-worth depends on their acceptance."

"My God, I am wearing a mask! I didn't even realize it!"

**The mask is not you**

The people of darkness kept telling me, "Get your act together! Prove yourself to us! Dance to the sound of our flute! Jump through our hoops!"

Their greatest compliment is to be referred to as a "class act"! Everyone in the domain of darkness is play-acting! Cap and Gown! Mask and Wig! Imposters! Pretend you're someone you're not!

## Appendix B: The Window

"I'm afraid to take this mask off! It's become so much a part of me!"

"Relax," a Person of Light says. "I'll help you. You can't remove it by yourself. None of us can! The Light you see coming from me is truth! The mask of darkness is a lie!

"We are not the Light! We are mortals from the domain of darkness just like you. Receive the Light that shines through us, and the mask will come off effortlessly. Does Light have your permission? Are you willing?"

"Yes, of course!"

I reach out. The mask is exposed and starts falling off! I grab it! Anxiety attack! About to panic! I've never felt like this before. I don't want to show who I really am! I'm not a lovable person! They wouldn't like me if they really knew me. I'm not worthy to come up to their platform. I really never have liked me! I've done many terrible things. I'm not good enough to go up there!

"No!" I scream! "I don't want to hear it! Being around you people makes me feel evil and stupid! I want to go back home, to the dope and games. I want to hide! Leave me alone!"

"Okay," responds a Person of Light.

"No one is allowed to insist that you come, but before you leave, please listen and consider. No person in darkness is good enough to come up here. We were all hiding behind a mask at one time or another in our lives.

"Even now, there's still a temptation for each of us to leave the platform and return to the dark world of pretense; but don't forget, the mask is a lie. You cannot hide from truth forever.

"Your body will soon breathe its last. The mask will come off, and, if you have rejected The Light of Truth, you will be helplessly lost in a dreadful darkness of agonizing torment! The consequence of living a lie!

"There's hope for you now, but there will never be hope behind that mask!"

Another person of light continues, "Access to the platform and Window is possible only through Mercy and Grace, which are expressions of disinterested love, that is, Love with no hidden agenda.

"God Almighty, Who is Love, loves you just as you are, even if you leave the mask on! You will never, ever be rejected here. Love is here to embrace you, the real you, who has been hiding behind the mask.

"Don't be afraid. The Light is Love, and Love has made the way and provided the helpers to help you come, if you are willing. I understand your reservations. I felt the same way. But believe me. Freedom awaits you.

"Come on up, and look out the Window for yourself! You'll never be the same! What your heart has been longing for has been waiting for you.

"Let me help you up. But remember! No masks allowed!"

I reach up and begin to feel the mask drop off! At first, I feel awkward, even exposed and naked. I look around me, and there are literally thousands, if not hundreds of thousands of discarded masks piled up all around the base of the platform.

The Person of Light takes my hand. Instantly, I'm on the Platform. There's a tremendous applause. People of Light are all around me, hugging me. They care for me, the real me!

**1 Peter 2:9:** I've been transferred out of the domain of darkness into the Kingdom of Light!

"No more games! No more dope! No more pretending! Come to the Window, and look for yourself," my new friend says.

She takes my hand and leads me. My heart is racing with the eerie sense of anticipation! Why would someone like me be allowed to look through this beautiful, awesome, majestic Window?

## Appendix B: The Window

I raise my head and look! There He is! An indescribable peace overcomes me. I forget all about myself.

OH, MY GOD! OH, MY GOD!
WE'RE FLYING TOWARD HIM!
HIS ARMS ARE OPEN!
HIS SMILE RADIATES LOVE AND HOPE,
INSPIRATION AND ENTHUSIASM!
I ONCE WAS BLIND, BUT NOW I SEE!
*EYE CONTACT*!
NOW IT'S GETTING VERY, VERY PERSONAL.
WE MAKE *EYE CONTACT!*
I CAN SEE THAT HE CAN SEE INTO MY VERY SOUL,
AND THE LOVE I FEEL IS INDESCRIBABLE!
ALL BURDENS ROLLED AWAY!
CAREFREE! FORGIVEN!
I'M FINALLY FREE FROM ME!
ADORATION AND ADMIRATION!
JESUS CHRIST!
IN HIS PERFECT RADIANT GLORY,
THE SCARS REMAIN OBVIOUS!
NOT ONLY IN HIS OUTSTRETCHED HANDS
BUT ALSO THE JAGGED MARKS ON HIS FOREHEAD
WHERE THEY RIDICULED HIM
WITH THE NEEDLE-SHARP CROWN OF THORNS!
HE IS PERFECT, UNFAILING LOVE!
THE CHAINS OF SELF-CONSCIOUSNESS THAT HAVE BOUND
ME TO THIS WORLD ARE FINALLY BROKEN!
I DON'T EVEN HAVE TO THINK ABOUT ME!

**I'VE LOST MYSELF IN THE LIGHT
OF THE ONE WHO IS PERFECT LOVE.
LOVE IS OUR DESTINATION!
WOW! WORD OF WORSHIP! WOW!**

In the background, I can still hear the continuous roar of overlapping conversations. The hearts of the people of darkness speaking, boasting, cursing, criticizing, shifting blame, and finding fault, and I realize for the first time that it no longer has any credibility:

> *"He said, she said, we said, they said; does it really matter what's said? Voices come and voices go. You're born, and then you're dead. But there is one solitary voice speaking from Heaven above: He says, "Deny yourself and follow Me. Your destination is LOVE!"*

Now that I have seen a glimpse of Jesus, His love is compelling me to reach out to those who are still in darkness and share the hope I've found, to be a channel of His Light, to help others who are ready to come to the Window.

I turn toward the crowd, and my perception has completely changed! All inclination toward fault finding, criticism, and blame shifting is no longer a part of me. My personal gavel has been broken and discarded.

I still see the pain, the shame, the shattered lives, the pretense, and physical death. My heart still breaks but not without hope. I pray everyone will one day be willing to drop their masks and come to the Window!

# Appendix B: The Window

As I observe the people in darkness from this new perspective, I notice that they have painted something on the inside wall of the spacecraft. A crowd gathers around the painting. What is it?

As I look more closely, I notice that those who have crowded around the painting seem to be more miserable, frightened, angry, and confused than the others!

The Light allows me to see more clearly. The painting on the wall is a painting of the Window! It looks so much like the Window, but it's a painting! Inside the painted window is a painted likeness of Jesus.

Oh, my God! The crowd is bowing down to the painting! They even bow to pictures and statues of the painters who died many years ago!

"God, it's so sad! It must break Your heart! You have made the way for each of us to see You, to know You, to live in Your Light, but most are afraid and refuse to remove their masks. They keep pretending and bowing to the counterfeit!

**2 Timothy 3:5** . . . holding on to a form of Godliness that has no power.

They are not being transformed. They are becoming more and more consumed by the darkness! Another deadly expression of pretense!

**The spacecraft is Planet Earth!**
**The crowd is lost humanity, the people of darkness.**

Violence, drug addiction, terrorism, suicide, murder, child molestation, rape, assault, and every imaginable and unimaginable form of perversion and social decay is escalating, the obvious symptoms of a spiritually blind species of beings who call themselves human beings. *Human beings being human beings!*

## The Window in Scripture:

**2 Corinthians 3:18:** "But we all, with unveiled face beholding as in a mirror the Glory of the Lord are being transformed into the same image from Glory to Glory even as by the Spirit of the Lord"

**Isaiah 45:22:** "Look unto Me and be saved all ye ends of the earth. I am God and there is no other!"

## Just Look

*I can't make myself believe in someone I can't see.*
*I can't make myself pretend to be*
*somebody other than me.*
*I can't make myself believe in a world of make-believe.*
*I'd rather quit than be a hypocrite.*
*I prayed a prayer with you, you even baptized me.*
*But nothing changed.*
*Everything remained the same,*
*As lost and confused as I could be.*
*So tired, so weak*
*Too tired to even seek.*
*That's what it took for me to Just Look.*

*Just Look, Just Look*
*Just Look and you will see,*
*The Truth, The Truth*
*The Truth that will set you free.*
*Just Look, Just Look*

## Appendix B: The Window

*Just Look and you will find*
*The missing piece to the puzzle of life,*
*Peace of mind. Just Look.*

*Seeing is believing the Truth in the midst of the lies.*
*Seeing is believing, the Lamb of God was crucified.*
*Soaked in His own blood*
*On a cross He was cursed and died.*
*That's what it took.*
*Just Look*

In Our Father's Arms,
Love,
Bob McLeod
1 Corinthians 13: 8

www.ingramcontent.com/pod-product-compliance
Lightning Source LLC
Chambersburg PA
CBHW021429080526
44588CB00009B/473